Kindergarten

Common Core State Standards
K- Lesson Plans

Kindergarten – Language Arts & Math

Teacher's Life

www.myteacherslife.com

Kindergarten

Table of Contents

Suggested Reading   7
Reading Language Arts   9
    RL.K.1
        First Day   10
        Bad Days   11
    RL.K.2
        My Version   13
        What Happens Next?   15
    RL.K.3
        Who Are We?   18
        Where Are We?   19
    RL.K.4
        What Is Meant   20
        Nonsense, Pure Nonsense   21
    RL.K.5
        1,2,3…Go   23
        Story or Poem   25
    RL.K.6
        Author or Illustrator   26
        Who Does What?   28
    RL.K.7
        What's Happening?   29
        Draw What's Important   30
    RL.K.9
        What Are They Like?   31
        What's Different?   32
    RI.K.1
        Bread   33
        Life Cycle of a Pumpkin   35
    RI.K.2
        My Main Topic   37
        Total Recall   38
    RI.K.3
        I Don't Know Why….   39
        Building Houses   44
    RI.K.4
        Label Me   46
        Draw An Alien   48

RI.K.5
- Show Me — 50
- Make A Book — 51

RI.K.6
- Stand Up, Sit Down — 53
- Library Rush — 54

RI.K.7
- Job Match — 55
- What Belongs? — 57

RI.K.8
- Support Beams — 59
- Show Your Support — 61

RI.K.9
- What's Different — 63
- Other Half — 65

RF.K.1
- What Letter Is Next? — 67
- What's A Word? — 69

RF.K.2
- Sounds Like… — 71
- Pull A Word — 75

RF.K.3
- Who Let the Letters Out? — 78
- Sight Word Scramble — 80

W.K.1
- My Favorite… — 82
- This Was Better — 84

W.K.2
- All About Me — 86
- All About Animals — 89

W.K.3
- Share With Me — 90
- And Then… — 92

W.K.5
- Build Me A Story — 94
- I'm Going to Need More Detail — 95

W.K.6
- Paint Me Some Pictures — 97
- What's in a Name? — 98

W.K.7
- I Think… — 99
- Art Explosion — 100

W.K.8
Tell Me About A Time When…	101
What Did You Have?	102

SL.K.1
Rules of the Talk	103
Talk About It	104

SL.K.2
Recycle This	106
Make It A Game	108

SL.K.3
What Do You Do?	109
Answer Me This	110

SL.K.4
My Bedroom	111
Fire Escape	112

SL.K.5
Finish This Drawing	113
Add to Me	115

SL.K.6
Pledge	117
Something Special	118

L.K.1
Written Pairs	119
Interrogation	121

L.K.2
Name This	123
Correct This	124

L.K.4
Duck or Duck	125
A Wave for You	127

L.K.5
Opposite Of	131
Sort It Out	133

Mathematics — 135

K.CC.1
Count On Me	136
100's Day	137

K.CC.2
You Can Count On Me	138
Count It Up	139

K.CC.3
Taking the Test	140

Kindergarten

Write and Wipe	141
K.CC.4	
One On One	142
How Many	144
K.CC.5	
Count Me Out	146
Mark It Out	147
K.CC.6	
Are There More?	149
Make This Bigger	150
K.CC.7	
Feed The Mathigator	151
Point Me in the Right Direction	153
K.OA.1	
Stomp It Out	154
Magic Math	155
K.OA.2	
Draw It Out	157
Show Me How It Goes	159
K.OA.3	
And ___ Makes 10	161
Slap Me Ten	163
K.OA.4	
Roll 'Em Up	164
Magnet Math	165
K.OA.5	
Minute Math Race	166
Sweet Subtraction	168
K.NBT.1	
Pick Me, Pick Me	169
Line It Up	171
K.MD.1	
How Do I Measure Up?	172
Wait on the Weight	173
K.MD.2	
String Theory	174
Build Them Up or Down	175
K.MD.3	
Sort It Out	176
Kid Sort	177
K.G.1	
Find A Place	178

Kindergarten

	Where Is The…	179
K.G.2		
	My Name Is…	180
	Shape Up	181
K.G.3		
	Shape Flattering Design	182
	Flat or Full Figured	184
K.G.4		
	Talk About Shapely	185
	Draw It Up	186
K.G.5		
	Model For Me	187
	Pick A Shape	188
K.G.6		
	Two + Two = Square	189
	Follow the Pattern	190

Suggested Reading
Literature

- Alexander and the Terrible, Horrible, No Good, Very Bad Day by Judith Viorst
- Bark, George by Jules Feiffer
- Caps for Sale by Esphyr Slobodkina
- Chicka Chicka Boom Boom by Martin and Archambault
- Click, Clack, Moo: Cows that Type by Doreen Cronin
- Curious George by H.A. Rey
- Danny and the Dinosaur by Syd Hoff
- Don't Let the Pigeon Drive the Bus! by Mo Willems
- George and Martha by James Marshall
- Green Eggs and Ham by Dr. Seuss
- If You Give A Mouse A Cookie by Laura Numeroff
- Miss Bindergarten Gets Ready for Kindergarten by Joseph Slate
- The Paper Bag Princess by Robert Munsch
- Strega Nona by Tomie De Paola
- Stellaluna by Janell Cannon

- Where The Wild Things Are by Maurice Sendak

Poetry

- An Alphabet by Edward Lear
- The Baby Dance by Ann Taylor
- What Does The Bee Do? by Christina Rossetti
- How to Paint a Donkey by Naomi Nye
- Daddy Fell Into the Pond by Alfred Noyes
- The Dentist and the Crocodile by Ronald Dahl
- What You Are You Are by Gwendolyn Brooks
- The Tyger by William Blake

Informational Test

- Seed, Sprout, Pumpkin Pie by Jill Esbaum
- What is a Triangle by Scholastic
- Animals Should Definitely Not Wear Clothing by Barrett
- The Magic School Bus Gets Recycled by Joanna Cole
- How A House is Built by Gail Gibbons
- A Day with Firefighters by Jan Kottke

Reading Language Arts

RL.K.1: Lesson One

Title: First Day

Topic: Retelling events

Objective of lesson: Students will correctly recall details in a text.

Common Core State Standard used: RL.K .1 With prompting and support, ask and answer questions about key details in a text.

Materials needed:

Heart stickers

Text: *The Kissing Hand* by Audrey Penn

Time for lesson: 15-20 minutes

Lesson

- Tell students you are going to read a book about the first day of school for a little raccoon.
- Ask students how they felt on their first day of school. Allow time for answers.
- Read the text out loud to all students.
- Ask various questions about the text, but do not ask what the mother drew on Chester's hand.
- As a final question have the whole class answer at the same time: What did Chester's mother draw on his paw?
- Place a small heart sticker on each child's hand as a reminder of the book.

Assessment: Correct answers

RL.K.1: Lesson Two

Title: Bad Days

Topic: Retelling events

Objective of lesson: Students will correctly recall details in a text.

Common Core State Standard used: RL.K .1 With prompting and support, ask and answer questions about key details in a text.

Materials needed:

Paper with boxes (at least six per sheet)

Crayons

Text: *Alexander and the Terrible, Horrible, No Good, Very Bad Day* by Judith Viorst

Time for lesson: 15-20 minutes

Lesson

- Tell students you are going to read a book about a little boy who had a very bad day.
- Explain to students that there is at least one line you would like them to help with during the book, but that they will figure that out as you read.
- Read the text *Alexander and the Terrible, Horrible, No Good, Very Bad Day*. Allow the students to read along if they can remember the repeated line.
- After reading the book, allow students to move to an area where they can draw.

Kindergarten

- In the first box on the paper have them draw the first 'bad' thing that happened to Alexander. Continue through six events. Use the book as a reminder if needed.
- On the back of the paper have students draw what happens when they have a bad day.

Assessment: Appropriate pictures

RL.K.2: Lesson One

Title: My Version

Topic: Retelling stories

Objective of lesson: Students will correctly retell familiar stories.

Common Core State Standard used: RL.K .2: With prompting and support, retell familiar stories, including key details

Materials Needed:

Paper that is partially lined and has an open space for drawing at the top.

Crayons

Text: *Cloudy with a Chance of Meatballs* by Judy Barrett

Time for lesson: 15-20 minutes

Lesson (Best if completed in small groups)

- Split students into groups of three or four, depending on class size.
- Tell students in the group that you are going to read them a funny book and read aloud the text.
- Have students discuss some of the major events.
- Tell students in the open space on the paper that they are going to draw a picture about the story and have them start.
- Work with one student at a time and have them retell the story for you as you write what they are saying verbatim. Repeat with all students.

Assessment: Appropriate pictures and retelling.

RL.K.2: Lesson Two

Title: What Happens Next?

Topic: Retelling stories

Objective of lesson: Students will correctly retell familiar parts of stories.

Common Core State Standard used: RL.K .2 Materials needed: With prompting and support, retell familiar stories, including key details

Materials Needed:

Popsicle stick puppets (Shapes included)

Text: *Polar Bear, Polar Bear What do You See?* By Eric Carle

Time for lesson: 15-20 minutes

Lesson

- Share the book *Polar Bear, Polar Bear What do You See?* Have students pay close attention to the order in which the animals/people are seen.
- After reading the book, hand out an animal, glued to a popsicle stick, to each student. (This can be done more than once to include all students or have two sets printed up)
- Begin reading the book again and as each animal comes up, have students with that animal stand up and march around the room, until all animals are marching.

Assessment: Correct retelling in order/Participation

Kindergarten

Polar Bear, Polar Bear samples:

Kindergarten

Kindergarten

RL.K.3: Lesson One

Title: Who Are We?

Topic: Identifying characters

Objective of lesson: Students will identify the characters in a story.

Common Core State Standard used: RL.K .3: With prompting and support, identify characters, settings, and major events in a story.

Materials Needed:

Paper

Crayons

Text: *The Mitten* by Jan Brett

Time for lesson: 15-30 minutes

Lesson

- Explain to students that characters are people or creatures in the story that have an important part. Some characters talk or sing, but all have human like thoughts, feelings, or voices.
- Read the story *The Mitten*. This book has numerous characters that are animals, that all try to fit into a mitten.
- Have students choose a character and draw a picture of it.
- Have students write the name of the character at the top. Help with spelling if necessary or have them sound it out.
- Post pictures.

Assessment: Picture of an actual character.

RL.K.3: Lesson Two

Title: Where Are We?

Topic: Identifying setting

Objective of lesson: Students will identify the setting(s) in a story.

Common Core State Standard used: RL.K.3: With prompting and support, identify characters, settings, and major events in a story.

Materials Needed:

Paper

Crayons

Text: *Where the Wild Things Are* by Maurice Sendak

Time for lesson: 15-30 minutes

Lesson

- Explain to students that a setting is where the action takes place in a story. Tell students that a story always has at least one setting, but it can have more than one also.

- Read the text *Where the Wild Things Are* to the class as a whole.

- Discuss the settings in the text with the students.

- Have students identify and then draw their favorite setting in the story and include a one or two word description of the setting.

Assessment: Picture of an actual setting.

RL.K.4: Lesson One

Title: What Is Meant?

Topic: Identifying new word meanings

Objective of lesson: Students will ask and answer questions about unfamiliar words.

Common Core State Standard used: RL.K.4: Ask and answer questions about unknown words in a text

Materials Needed:

Chart paper

Markers

Text: *Verdi* by Janell Cannon

Time for lesson: 10-15 minutes

Lesson

- Have students gather in a large group to listen to the story *Verdi*
- After each page, ask students if there are any words they did not recognize. If so, record those words on chart paper.
- If a word is not recognized, have students turn it into a question. What does the word... mean?
- Have another student answer.

Assessment: Participation

RL.K.4: Lesson Two

Title: Nonsense, Pure Nonsense

Topic: Identifying new word meanings

Objective of lesson: Students will ask and answer questions about unfamiliar words.

Common Core State Standard used: RL.K.4: Ask and answer questions about unknown words in a text

Materials Needed:

Sample sentences (Included)

Paper

Crayons

Time for lesson: 10-15 minutes (depending on number of sentences used)

Lesson

- Explain to students that you are going to read sentences one at a time and that the sentences will have one strange word in it.

- Offer the following example: The flopter grew up from the ground and had five red petals. Ask students what a flopter might be. (Flower).

- As you read each sentence with nonsense word, have students draw what the word should mean for each sentence.

Assessment: Appropriate pictures

Sample sentences:

The children rode the *slider* down the snow in the winter. (Sled)

The *picturebobber* played cartoon every afternoon. (Television)

The *treberbob* was covered in beautiful yellow leaves that would all fall off in a few weeks because it would be autumn. (Tree)

The *slitherpop* moved quickly across the road. Lots of people are afraid of *slitherpops* because they think they are slimy, but they are not. (Snake)

The *twinklelibs* are out tonight and look like little lights in the sky. (Stars)

The *flupperpup* was brown and white and barked when cars went by. (Dog)

I brushed my *lockerflop* after my shower because it was all over my head. (Hair)

I keep my *chomperdots* well cared for so the dentist does not have to pull any of them. (teeth)

The *timerplot* ticked away each second of everyminute, all day long. (Clock)

I put *fluppersoppers* on my feet to keep them warm. I even have *fluppersoppers* that are striped and have polkadots. (Socks or slippers)

RL.K.5: Lesson One

Title: 1,2,3....Go

Topic: Identifying text types

Objective of lesson: Students will identify specific types of texts

Common Core State Standard used: RL.K .5: Recognize common types of texts (e.g., storybooks, poems)

Materials Needed:

Tubs (Included)

Selection of books and prints (Newspaper, Magazine, Reference, Storybook, Poems)

Time for lesson: 5-15 minutes

Lesson

- Explain and offer an example of the different types of texts listed above.

- After explanation, place the samples in different parts of the room.

- Hand each student a slip of paper with a type of text on it (Included)

- On the count of three, have students move to the area that contains their type of text.

- Repeat as desired.

Assessment: Accuracy/Participation

Newspaper

Magazine

Reference

Storybook

Poem

RL.K.5: Lesson Two

Title: Story or Poem

Topic: Identifying text types

Objective of lesson: Students will identify specific types of texts

Common Core State Standard used: RL.K.5: Recognize common types of texts (e.g., storybooks, poems)

Materials Needed:

Story books

Poetry collection books

Time for lesson: 5-15 minutes

Lesson

- Explain the difference between a poem and a story to students.
- Read a sample from each type of book to show students.
- Now, place both books on your lap and have students turn their back to you.
- Read a selection from one book and have students raise the right hand for poetry and the left hand for storybook.

Assessment: Accuracy/Participation

RL.K.6: Lesson One

Title: Author and Illustrator

Topic: Identifying author and illustrator

Objective of lesson: Students will find the author and illustrator in a book

Common Core State Standard used: RL.K .6: With prompting and support, name the author and illustrator of a story and define the role of each in telling the story.

Materials Needed

Several copies of book covers with author and illustrators

Dry erase in two covers for each child

Sheet protectors

Time for lesson: 5 minutes (per small group)

Lesson

- Show children the sample cover of the book and explain how to find the author and illustrator.
- Hand each child a copy of a book cover (all different if possible) in sheet protector.
- Have students highlight the author in one color and illustrator in another

Assessment: Accuracy/Participation

Kindergarten

RL.K.6: Lesson Two

Title: Who Does What?

Topic: Identifying author and illustrator

Objective of lesson: Students will identify the job of both the author and illustrator.

Common Core State Standard used: RL.K .6: With prompting and support, name the author and illustrator of a story and define the role of each in telling the story.

Materials Needed:

Several copies of book covers with author and illustrators

Time for lesson: 2 minutes before each reading

Lesson

- Choose several books to share throughout the week. Make sure each book has both an author and illustrator.

- Before reading ask students to identify where to find the author and ask what the author does. Do the same with the illustrator.

Assessment: Participation

RL.K.7: Lesson One

Title: What's Happening?

Topic: Identify the part of the story that is illustrated

Objective of lesson: Students will identify the part of a passage that is illustrated

Common Core State Standard used: RL.K .7: With prompting and support, describe the relationship between illustrations and the story in which they appear (e.g., what moment in a story an illustration depicts).

Materials Needed:

Text: *The Berestain Bears series* by Jan Berenstain

Time for lesson: 5-15 minutes

Lesson (Small or large groups)

- Explain to students that not everything that is written can have a picture to go with it or books would all be very, very long.

- Begin reading one of *The Berestain Bears* books. After each reading, ask different students what part is being shown in the picture.

Assessment: Participation/Accuracy

RL.K.7: Lesson Two

Title: Draw What's Important

Topic: Identify the most important part of the story to illustrate

Objective of lesson: Students will identify the part of a passage that is likely to be illustrated

Common Core State Standard used: RL.K .7: With prompting and support, describe the relationship between illustrations and the story in which they appear (e.g., what moment in a story an illustration depicts).

Materials Needed:

Text: *The Berestain Bears series* by Jan Berenstain

Time for lesson: 5-15 minutes

Lesson (Small or large groups)

- Begin reading *The Berestain Bears* series to students, but do not show the pictures.
- After reading the first page, ask students what the most important thing that happened was.
- If that is the most important thing, then the picture (illustration) probably represents that part.
- Allow students to check their guesses by looking at the picture.

Assessment: Participation/Accuracy

RL.K.9: Lesson One

Title: What Are They Like?

Topic: Comparing characters

Objective of lesson: Students will compare and contrast characters in a story

Common Core State Standard used: RL.K.9: With prompting and support, compare and contrast the adventures and experiences of characters in familiar stories.

Materials Needed:

Text: *The Junie B. Jones kindergarten series* by Barbara Parks

Time for lesson: 10-20 minutes (per day, over time)

Lesson

- Begin reading *The Junie B. Jones* series to students, chapter by chapter.

- As characters are introduced, make lists of words to describe them

- As you read on, stop to ask students what a particular character is likely to do in the given situation.

- Allow students time to offer scenarios and then check to see if they were right by reading on

Assessment: Participation

RL.K.9: Lesson Two

Title: What's Different?

Topic: Comparing characters in two similar books

Objective of lesson: Students will compare and contrast characters in similar stories

Common Core State Standard used: RL.K.9: With prompting and support, compare and contrast the adventures and experiences of characters in familiar stories.

Materials Needed:

Text: *Three Little Javelinas* by Susan Lowell

Three Little Pigs by Author of Your Choice

Time for lesson: 10-20 minutes

Lesson

- Tell students that you are going to read two stories that are very similar and you want them to pay close attention.

- Read each book, allowing students to discuss as you read.

- Draw a Venn diagram on the board and allow students to come up with similarities and differences as you record them for the class.

Assessment: Participation

RI.K.1: Lesson One

Title: Bread

Topic: Answering questions

Objective of lesson: Students will ask and answer questions about key details in a story

Common Core State Standard used: RI.K .1: With prompting and support, ask and answer questions about key details in a text.

Materials Needed:

Text: *Bread, Bread, Bread* by Ann Morris

Sheet protectors with card stock inserted (Dry erase board)

Dry erase markers

Paper towels (Erasers)

Time for lesson: 10-20 minutes

Lesson

- Tell students that you are going to read a book about different types of bread.
- Read the text.
- Ask students questions about the book and have them wither draw or write a one word answer on their boards.
- After each question have students hold up boards for quick checking.

Assessment: Participation/Correct answers

RI.K.1: Lesson Two

Title: Life Cycle of a Pumpkin

Topic: Answering questions based on a text

Objective of lesson: Students will ask and answer questions about key details in a story

Common Core State Standard used: RI.K.1: With prompting and support, ask and answer questions about key details in a text.

Materials Needed:

Text: *Seed, Sprout, Pumpkin, Pie* by Jill Esbaum

Paper folded into four squares

Crayons

Scissors

Time for lesson: 10-30 minutes

Lesson

- Read the text to students, drawing attention to the pictures of the four main steps: seeds, sprouts, pumpkin, pie
- Have students use each box on their paper to draw one of the steps.
- Have students cut apart each box
- Mix up boxes and ask students to retell each step by putting the boxes in order.

Assessment: Participation/Correct answers

RI.K.2: Lesson One

Title: My Main Topic

Topic: Identifying main topic of a book

Objective of lesson: Students will learn to identify the main topic

Common Core State Standard used: RI.K.2: With prompting and support, identify the main topic and retell key details of a text.

Materials Needed:

Selection of informational texts (See list)

Time for lesson: 5-10 minutes

Lesson

- Display several informational books in an area that students can view them.

- Explain that most times the main topic of the book is as easy as reading the title.

- Have students look at each title and picture and decide what the main topic may be.

- Remind students that main topics are what a book is about and are only one or two words long.

Assessment: Participation

RI.K.2: Lesson Two

Title: Total Recall

Topic: Identifying key points in a text

Objective of lesson: Students will learn to retell key details

Common Core State Standard used: RI.K.2: With prompting and support, identify the main topic and retell key details of a text.

Materials Needed:

Text: *The Tiny Seed* by Eric Carle

Plastic cups

Soil

Seeds

Time for lesson: 10-20 minutes

Lesson

- Read the text to all students.
- Ask students what happened first, second, third, etc.
- Allow students to plant their own tiny seeds in cups of dirt to watch the book come alive.

Assessment: Participation/Correct answers

RI.K.3: Lesson One

Title: I Don't Know Why...

Topic: Connecting events

Objective of lesson: Students will learn to retell key details

Common Core State Standard used: RI.K .3: With prompting and support, describe the connection between two individuals, events, ideas, or pieces of information in a text.

Materials Needed:

Text: *There was an Old Lady Who Swallowed a Fly* by Simms Taback

Sandwich bags

Tape

Story parts (Included)

Scissors

Crayons

Time for lesson: 10-20 minutes

Lesson

- Read the text to all students.
- Have students color the woman's head and then tape (or staple) the head to the baggie (head at open part)
- Have students color story parts

- As you read the book a second time have students 'feed' the appropriate part to the woman.

- Ask students why each part is necessary (Spider to catch fly...etc.)

Assessment: Participation

Kindergarten

Kindergarten

RI.K.3: Lesson Two

Title: Building Houses

Topic: Connecting events

Objective of lesson: Students will learn to retell key details

Common Core State Standard used: RI.K.3: With prompting and support, describe the connection between two individuals, events, ideas, or pieces of information in a text.

Materials Needed:

Text: *How a House is Built* by Gail Gibbons

House pieces (Included: Door, two windows, house, roof)

Glue

Scissors

Crayons

Time for lesson: 10-20 minutes

Lesson

- Read the text to students.
- Ask students basic questions such as: What would happen if the roof was built first? or What happens if there is a door, but no walls?

Kindergarten

- **Next have students put together their house in the right order. Keep asking what comes next and pay attention to make sure students are creating in the right order.**
- **Allow students to color and display projects.**

Assessment: Participation/Correct house

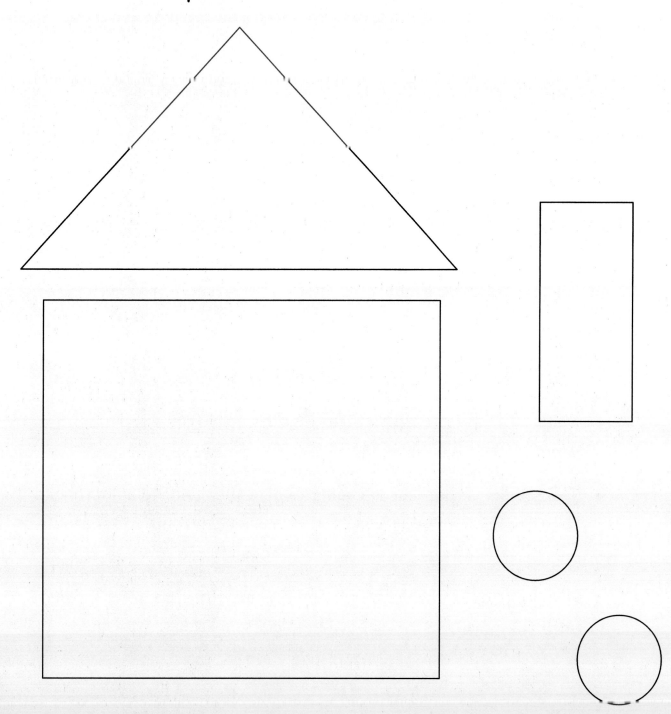

RI.K.4: Lesson One

Title: Label Me

Topic: Identifying the unknown

Objective of lesson: Students will label fruits and vegetables using correct terms.

Common Core State Standard used: RI.K .4: With prompting and support, ask and answer questions about unknown words in a text.

Materials Needed:

Selection of fruits and vegetables (or pictures of them)

Cards with names (Some included)

Time for lesson: 10-20 minutes

Lesson

- Tell students that you are going to work with some new big words.

- Show all the displayed pictures of different fruits and vegetables.

- Tell students that you are going to give them individual hints and they are going to use their label to mark each fruit or vegetable correctly. This way they can learn the new word.

- Give hints as to the vegetable/fruit name the student is holding until they can guess it or have help guessing it.

Kindergarten

- Allow student to place the label and read it. Congratulate them on 'reading' such a large word.

Assessment: Participation

Cucumber	Peach
Carrot	Apple
Lettuce	Banana
Potato	Watermelon
Corn	Cantaloupe
Broccoli	Pear
Tomato	Pineapple
Cauliflower	Pomegranate

RI.K.4: Lesson Two

Title: Draw an Alien

Topic: Identifying unknown words in context

Objective of lesson: Students will identify unknown words in context

Common Core State Standard used: RI.K .4: With prompting and support, ask and answer questions about unknown words in a text.

Materials Needed:

Alien description

Crayons

Paper

Time for lesson: 5 -10 minutes

Lesson

- Tell students they are going to draw an alien as you read about its different parts. Explain that some words may not make sense, but that they need to try to figure out and draw in the right place.
- Read the poem. Tell students to pay close attention to the details
- Observe as students draw.

Assessment: Correct picture as described

Alien Description

The large green alien had six flibbertygibbets, three on each side.

All the flibbertygibbets had four fingers each.

The alien also had large purple flapports

One of which had a yellow sock on it

On top of its head was a patch of red flyerway.

Its orbals were bright blue, and it had three on its face

A tiny pink nostrilsome sat in the middle of its face and it snorted as the alien moved.

Its smile was monsterous with dripping black gripperfangs that looked like they could chew through a tree.

Show me your aliens!

RI.K.5: Lesson One

Title: Show Me

Topic: Identifying book parts

Objective of lesson: Students will identify parts of a book

Common Core State Standard used: RI.K.5: Identify the front cover, back cover, and title page of a book.

Materials Needed:

Several books

Time for lesson: 5-10 minutes

Lesson

- Display several books in front of the class.

- Have students come up one at a time and ask one of three questions: Where is the front of the book?, Where is the back of the book?, What or where is the title of the book? Help students as needed.

Assessment: Correct identification

RI.K.5: Lesson Two

Title: Make a Book

Topic: Identifying book parts

Objective of lesson: Students will identify parts of a book

Common Core State Standard used: RI.K.5: Identify the front cover, back cover, and title page of a book.

Materials Needed:

Three sheets of paper per child

Stapler

Crayons

Time for lesson: 10-20 minutes

Lesson

- Offer each student three sheets of paper and have them fold the sheets in half to create a 'book'.

- Staple along the edges of the book so that it now has a spine.

- Ask students to put a title on the book. It can be anything appropriate they choose or you can write a title on the board for them to copy.

- Next, have students write their name where an author's name could be.

- Finally, have students label the back of the book. The goal is that they label the book as if it were real, in the correct places.

- Allow students to fill the pages with drawings or a story they invent on their own of as a class.

Assessment: Correct placement of book parts

RI.K.6: Lesson One

Title: Stand Up, Sit Down

Topic: Understanding author and illustrator

Objective of lesson: Students will know the jobs of the author and illustrator

Common Core State Standard used: RI.K.6: Name the author and illustrator of a text and define the role of each in presenting the ideas or information in a text.

Materials Needed:

Time for lesson: 5 minutes

Lesson

- Tell students you are going to play a very quick game to wake them up a little. Have students seated in chairs.

- Explain that when you ask a question if the answer is author then the student is to stand up, but if it is illustrator, they are to sit on the floor.

- Ask several questions such as: Who writes the words?; Who draws the pictures?; Who's name is usually first on the book?; What does every book have?; etc

Assessment: Observation

RI.K.6: Lesson Two

Title: Library Rush

Topic: Understanding author and illustrator

Objective of lesson: Students will know how to check if an author and illustrator are listed on a book.

Common Core State Standard used: RI.K .6: Name the author and illustrator of a text and define the role of each in presenting the ideas or information in a text.

Materials Needed:

Access to a library

Time for lesson: 5-15 minutes

Lesson

- Remind students of how to locate the author and illustrator on a book cover.
- Tell students you are going to visit the library and review library rules.
- Once in library have students search for books for books that have both an author and illustrator.

Assessment: Finding an appropriate book

RI.K.7: Lesson One

Title: Job Match

Topic: Understanding relationships

Objective of lesson: Students will connect professionals to parts of their job

Common Core State Standard used: RI.K.7: With prompting and support, describe the relationship between illustrations and the text in which they appear (e.g., what person, place, thing, or idea in the text an illustration depicts).

Materials Needed:

Text: *ABC of Jobs* by Roger Priddy

Matching pictures (Samples included)

Time for lesson: 10-20 minutes

Lesson (Small group lesson)

- Read the text to students.
- Allow students to attempt to match professionals to where they work or are most likely to be seen.

Assessment: Finding appropriate matches.

Kindergarten

RI.K.7: Lesson Two

Title: What Belongs?

Topic: Understanding relationships

Objective of lesson: Students will add appropriate items to pictures

Common Core State Standard used: RI.K.7: With prompting and support, describe the relationship between illustrations and the text in which they appear (e.g., what person, place, thing, or idea in the text an illustration depicts).

Materials Needed:

Peel and stick books or Pictures with missing elements (Samples included)

Time for lesson: 5-10 minutes

Lesson (Small group lesson)

- Show students a picture with certain elements missing. Ask students what might go in the spot.
- Have students draw appropriate picture parts in the empty boxes.

Assessment: Drawing of appropriate picture parts

Kindergarten 58

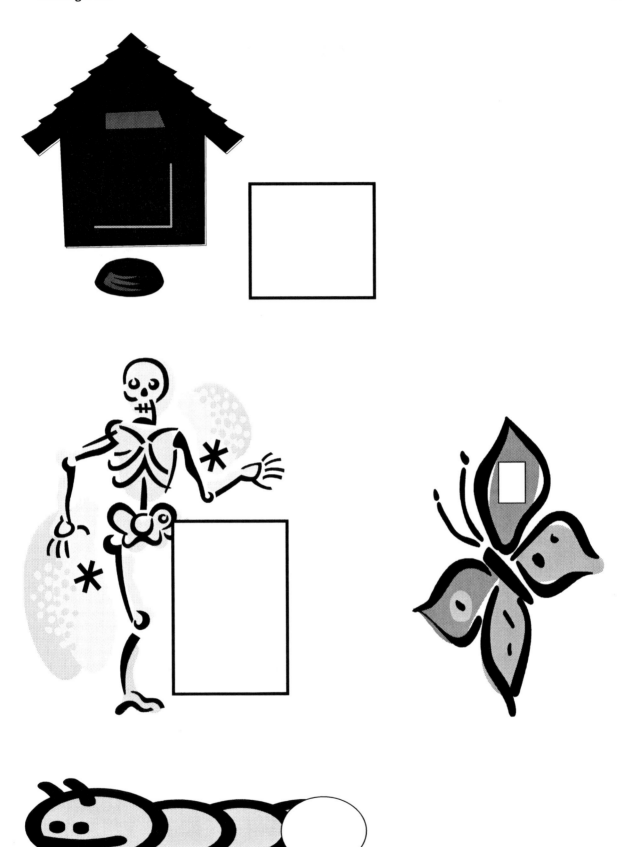

RI.K.8: Lesson One

Title: Support Beams

Topic: Supporting ideas

Objective of lesson: Students will create a hands-on example of supporting ideas

Common Core State Standard used: RI.K.8: With prompting and support, identify the reasons an author gives to support points in a text.

Materials Needed:

Building blocks that are not joinable, but are stackable (Lincoln logs, cardboard blocks)

Text: *How A House is Built* by Gail Gibbons

Time for lesson: 10-15 minutes

Lesson

- Split students into two groups or more if a large class
- Have half the groups use blocks to build a roof and half use blocks to build a house without a roof.
- Have students try to move the roof to set on top of the house. This should fail.
- Ask students what can be done to make building the project easier. (Work together)

- Explain to students that this is like an author supporting his ideas. The ideas must work together to present a clear picture.
- Share the text and see if students can find supporting ideas.

Assessment: Participation

RI.K.8: Lesson Two

Title: Show Your Support

Topic: Supporting ideas

Objective of lesson: Students will work as a class to show supporting parts of a text.

Common Core State Standard used: RI.K.8: With prompting and support, identify the reasons an author gives to support points in a text.

Materials Needed:

Text: *My Mom is a Firefighter* by Lois Grambling

Chart (Included)

Time for lesson: 10-15 minutes

Lesson

- Read the text to the class as a whole.
- Ask students to identify the main topic (Being a firefighter)
- Identify things in the book to support what being a firefighter is like.
- Place the supporting ideas in the chart

Assessment: Participation

Kindergarten

Main Idea:

RI.K.9: Lesson One

Title: What's Different?

Topic: Identifying differences

Objective of lesson: Students will find the differences in two similar pictures.

Common Core State Standard used: RI.K.9: With prompting and support, identify basic similarities in and differences between two texts on the same topic (e.g., in illustrations, descriptions, or procedures).

Materials Needed:

Pictures (Sample included)

Time for lesson: 5-10 minutes

Lesson

- Explain to students that sometimes we read two or three books that sound the same, but actually have different information.

- Tell students they are going to practice finding differences in pictures, before looking for them in books.

- Give each student a set of pictures and have them circle all the differences. (This is a great end of day or beginning of day activity.) Color the stars for each difference you find.

Assessment: Finding differences

Kindergarten

☆ ☆ ☆ ☆ ☆

☆ ☆ ☆ ☆ ☆

RI.K.9: Lesson Two

Title: Other Half

Topic: Identifying and creating similarities

Objective of lesson: Students will create an identical half of a picture

Common Core State Standard used: RI.K.9: With prompting and support, identify basic similarities in and differences between two texts on the same topic (e.g., in illustrations, descriptions, or procedures).

Materials Needed:

Pictures (Sample included)

Time for lesson: 5-10 minutes

Lesson

- Explain to students that when we read stories there is often information that is the same in both books. Things like both being about animals or both being about little girls.

- Explain that pictures are often the same way.

- Tell them that to practice seeing the same information in things, you are going to practice drawing identical sides of a drawing.

- Share the half-drawings with students and have them complete the other half.

Assessment: Creating an appropriate drawing

Kindergarten 66

RF.K.1: Lesson One

Title: What Letter is Next?

Topic: Demonstrate understanding of print organization

Objective of lesson: Students will organize letters appropriately

Common Core State Standard used: RF.K .1: Demonstrate understanding of the organization and basic features of print.

- Follow words from left to right, top to bottom, and page by page.
- Recognize that spoken words are represented in written language by specific sequences of letters.
- Understand that words are separated by spaces in print.
- Recognize and name all upper- and lowercase letters of the alphabet.

Materials Needed:

Alphabet order worksheet (Included)

Dry erase markers or pencils

Time for lesson: 5-10 minutes

Lesson

- If students are just learning letter organization then complete this as a class, otherwise, individual work is acceptable.
- Project the letter sequences onto the board.

- Allow students to volunteer to go write the missing letter in the space.

Assessment: Correct letter placement

Samples: (Add more as needed)

A __ C

F __ H

X __ Z

B __ D E F __ H I

L __ __ O P

__ R S T

A B C D E __ G H __ J K

__ B C D __ F G H __

X __ Z A __ C D __

D E F __ __ __ J K L __

RF.K.1: Lesson Two

Title: What's A Word?

Topic: Demonstrate understanding of print organization

Objective of lesson: Students show understanding of separate words

Common Core State Standard used: RF.K.1: Demonstrate understanding of the organization and basic features of print.

- Follow words from left to right, top to bottom, and page by page.
- Recognize that spoken words are represented in written language by specific sequences of letters.
- Understand that words are separated by spaces in print.
- Recognize and name all upper- and lowercase letters of the alphabet.

Materials Needed:

Highlighters (Two colors per child) or Highlighting tape

Worksheet of printed sentences

Time for lesson: 10-15 minutes

Lesson (Small groups)

- Offer students the worksheet of sentences.
- Tell students that words are always separated by spaces and they are going to highlight the separate words in each sentence.
- Allow students to alternate highlighters to show separate words.

Kindergarten

Assessment: Correct identification of separate words

Sample:

The dog ran beside the lake.

RF.K.2: Lesson One

Title: Sounds Like...

Topic: Rhyming words

Objective of lesson: Students will demonstrate an ability to rhyme

Common Core State Standard used: RF.K.2: Demonstrate understanding of spoken words, syllables, and sounds (phonemes).

- Recognize and produce rhyming words.

- Count, pronounce, blend, and segment syllables in spoken words.

- Blend and segment onsets and rimes of single-syllable spoken words.

- Isolate and pronounce the initial, medial vowel, and final sounds (phonemes) in three-phoneme (consonant-vowel-consonant, or CVC) words.[1] (This does not include CVCs ending with /l/, /r/, or /x/.)

- Add or substitute individual sounds (phonemes) in simple, one-syllable words to make new words.

Materials Needed:

Alphabet tiles (Paper samples included)

Time for lesson: 10-15 minutes

Lesson (Small groups)

- Give each student a set of alphabet tiles.

Kindergarten

- Help students in the group to spell out only an ending such as ime, it, at, og, un

- Help students sound out the ending and then show them how to add a letter to make a real or nonsense word.

- Explain that if the ending doesn't change, changing the first sound will create rhyming words.

- Have students see what rhyming words they can create.

Assessment: Creating real and nonsense rhyming words

A	B	C	D	E
F	G	H	I	J
K	L	M	N	O
P	Q	R	S	T
U	V	W	X	Y
Z	A	E	I	O
U				

Extra Letters

RF.K.2: Lesson One

Title: Sounds Like...

Topic: Rhyming words

Objective of lesson: Students will demonstrate an ability to rhyme

Common Core State Standard used: RF.K .2: Demonstrate understanding of spoken words, syllables, and sounds (phonemes).

- Recognize and produce rhyming words.

- Count, pronounce, blend, and segment syllables in spoken words.

- Blend and segment onsets and rimes of single-syllable spoken words.

- Isolate and pronounce the initial, medial vowel, and final sounds (phonemes) in three-phoneme (consonant-vowel-consonant, or CVC) words.[1] (This does not include CVCs ending with /l/, /r/, or /x/.)

- Add or substitute individual sounds (phonemes) in simple, one-syllable words to make new words.

Materials Needed:

Alphabet tiles (Paper samples included)

Time for lesson: 10-15 minutes

Lesson (Small groups)

- Give each student a set of alphabet tiles.

- Help students in the group to spell out only an ending such as ime, it, at, og, un

- Help students sound out the ending and then show them how to add a letter to make a real or nonsense word.

- Explain that if the ending doesn't change, changing the first sound will create rhyming words.

- Have students see what rhyming words they can create.

Assessment: Creating real and nonsense rhyming words

RF.K.2: Lesson Two

Title: Pull A Word

Topic: Initial sounds and CVC combinations

Objective of lesson: Students will demonstrate sounding out and reading CVC combinations

Common Core State Standard used: RF.K .2: Demonstrate understanding of spoken words, syllables, and sounds (phonemes).

- Recognize and produce rhyming words.

- Count, pronounce, blend, and segment syllables in spoken words.

- Blend and segment onsets and rimes of single-syllable spoken words.

- Isolate and pronounce the initial, medial vowel, and final sounds (phonemes) in three-phoneme (consonant-vowel-consonant, or CVC) words.[1] (This does not include CVCs ending with /l/, /r/, or /x/.)

- Add or substitute individual sounds (phonemes) in simple, one-syllable words to make new words.

Materials Needed:

Pull a word (Sample included)

Time for lesson: 10-15 minutes

Lesson (Small groups)

Kindergarten

- Help students create or use pull-a-word charts to practice initial sounds and CVC words.

- Have students sound out and read each word as an individual or small group.

Assessment: Reading and sounding out words.

un

Cut on dotted lines. Thread letter strip from back and into bottom slit, so that only one letter at a time is showing. Change word endings as needed or desired.

B
D
F
G
H
N
P
R
S
T
V
W

RF.K.3: Lesson One

Title: Who Let The Letters Out?

Topic: Letter/sound correspondence

Objective of lesson: Students will demonstrate letter/sound correspondence through song

Common Core State Standard used: RF.K.3: Know and apply grade-level phonics and word analysis skills in decoding words.

- Demonstrate basic knowledge of letter-sound correspondences by producing the primary or most frequent sound for each consonant.

- Associate the long and short sounds with the common spellings (graphemes) for the five major vowels.

- Read common high-frequency words by sight (e.g., *the, of, to, you, she, my, is, are, do, does*)

- Distinguish between similarly spelled words by identifying the sounds of the letters that differ.

Materials Needed:

Dr Jean cd or song: *Who Let the Letters Out*

Time for lesson: 3-5 minutes

Lesson

- Use the Dr. Jean cd and song to allow students to practice letter sound correspondence.

- Point to each letter as it is sang.
- If time permits use brown lunch bags and shred the open end, wad up the closed end, and create pompons for the students to cheer the letters with.

Assessment: Participation

RF.K.3: Lesson Two

Title: Sight Word Scramble

Topic: Recognition of sight words

Objective of lesson: Students will read common sight words

Common Core State Standard used: RF.K .3: Know and apply grade-level phonics and word analysis skills in decoding words.

- Demonstrate basic knowledge of letter-sound correspondences by producing the primary or most frequent sound for each consonant.

- Associate the long and short sounds with the common spellings (graphemes) for the five major vowels.

- Read common high-frequency words by sight (e.g., *the, of, to, you, she, my, is, are, do, does*).

- Distinguish between similarly spelled words by identifying the sounds of the letters that differ.

Materials Needed:

Plastic spatula for each small group

Copy of egg words (Sample included)

Time for lesson: 5-10 minutes

Lesson (Small groups)

- Give each group a spatula and a set of words.
- Tell students to turn the 'eggs' face side down.

- Taking turns have students flip over one egg at a time using the spatula and read the sight word they have overturned.

Assessment: Appropriate recognition of common sight words

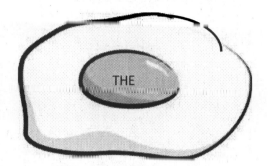 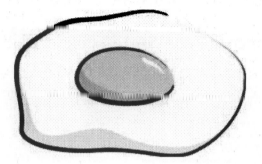

Change center word as needed or add more words.

W.K.1: Lesson One

Title: My Favorite...

Topic: Opinion pieces

Objective of lesson: Identifying opinions

Common Core State Standard used: W.K .1: Use a combination of drawing, dictating, and writing to compose opinion pieces in which they tell a reader the topic or the name of the book they are writing about and state an opinion or preference about the topic or book (e.g., *My favorite book is...*).

Materials Needed:

Paper (Worksheet included)

Selection of books for the week

Time for lesson: 5-15 minutes daily

Lesson

- Each day read a different style book each day for a week.
- On the final day have students choose a favorite from the ones read.
- Have students fill out the worksheet below and draw an accompanying picture. Student's can copy titles from the book.

Assessment: Appropriate pictures and writing.

Kindergarten

My favorite book this week was
_____

My favorite part of the book looked like this:

W.K.1: Lesson Two

Title: This Was Better

Topic: Opinion pieces

Objective of lesson: Identifying opinions about books

Common Core State Standard used: W.K .1: Use a combination of drawing, dictating, and writing to compose opinion pieces in which they tell a reader the topic or the name of the book they are writing about and state an opinion or preference about the topic or book (e.g., *My favorite book is...*).

Materials Needed:

Paper

Crayons

Selection of books for the week

Time for lesson: 5-15 minutes daily

Lesson

- Choose a text to read to the class as a whole.
- Read the text aloud.
- Have students fold a sheet of paper in have and copy the following labels off the board: Most Favorite, Least Favorite. One for each side.
- Have students draw a picture of their most and least favorite parts of the shared story.

Kindergarten

Assessment: Appropriate pictures

Most Favorite | **Least Favorite**

W.K.2: Lesson One

Title: All About Me

Topic: Informative writing/drawing

Objective of lesson: Creating informative writings and drawings

Common Core State Standard used: W.K .2: Use a combination of drawing, dictating, and writing to compose informative/explanatory texts in which they name what they are writing about and supply some information about the topic.

Materials Needed:

All About Me sheet (Included)

Crayons

Pencils

Time for lesson: 15-30 minutes

Lesson

- Tell students that they are going to write about something they know better than any other topic. About themselves.
- Read along with students to help them fill in each blank with a word or picture or both as outlined in the worksheet.
- Put booklet pages together and have students draw a picture of themselves on the outer cover.

Assessment: Appropriate pictures, answers, and writing

Kindergarten

My name is _____

My favorite color is _____

My favorite sport is

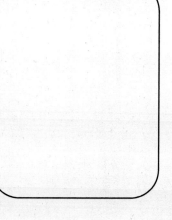   This is my favorite subject in school.

Kindergarten

My favorite animal is

My favorite thing to do is

is my favorite food.

I love

W.K.2: Lesson Two

Title: All About Animals

Topic: Informative writing/drawing

Objective of lesson: Creating informative writings and drawings

Common Core State Standard used: W.K.2: Use a combination of drawing, dictating, and writing to compose informative/explanatory texts in which they name what they are writing about and supply some information about the topic.

Materials Needed:

Text: *Animals A to Z* by David McPhail

Crayons

Pencils

Time for lesson: 15-30 minutes

Lesson

- Share the text with students in large or small groups.
- Discuss some of the facts presented in the book about animals.
- Have students choose an animal and draw a picture of that animal.
- Have students dictate one fact about the chosen animal as you write it on the paper.
- Have students try to copy the fact in their own writing

Assessment: Appropriate pictures, answers, and writing

W.K.3: Lesson One

Title: Share With Me

Topic: Sequential drawing

Objective of lesson: Students will create a sequential retelling of a text

Common Core State Standard used: W.K.3: Use a combination of drawing, dictating, and writing to narrate a single event or several loosely linked events, tell about the events in the order in which they occurred, and provide a reaction to what happened.

Materials Needed:

Text: *Rainbow Fish* by Marcus Pfister

Crayons

Comic strip or blocked paper

Time for lesson: 15-30 minutes

Lesson

- Share the text with students in large or small groups.
- Discuss what happens in order in the book
- Offer students the blocked paper and have them draw pictures about what was discussed. One scene should be presented in each box. (Beginning students can be asked to draw the beginning, middle, and end, but number of boxes can be increased throughout the year.)

Assessment: Appropriate pictures in sequential order.

W.K.3: Lesson Two

Title: And Then...

Topic: Sequential drawing and writing

Objective of lesson: Students will create a sequential retelling of a text

Common Core State Standard used: W.K .3: Use a combination of drawing, dictating, and writing to narrate a single event or several loosely linked events, tell about the events in the order in which they occurred, and provide a reaction to what happened.

Materials Needed:

Text: *If You Give A Mouse A Cookie* by Laura Numeroff

Crayons

Step Paper (Sample included)

Time for lesson: 15-30 minutes

Lesson

- Share the text with students in large or small groups.
- Explain to students that in the book, one thing led to another with the mouse.
- Have students write one word descriptions and draw pictures of each step in the book. (Sample included)

Assessment: Appropriate pictures and words in sequential order.

Kindergarten

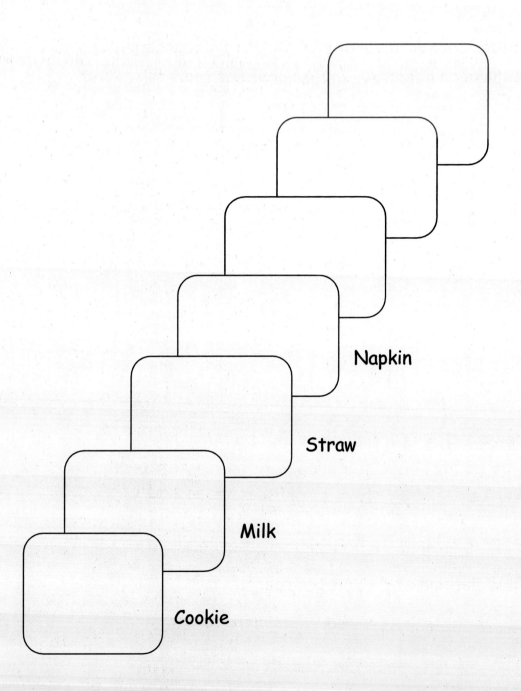

W.K.5: Lesson One

Title: Build Me A Story

Topic: Strengthening writing

Objective of lesson: Students will work together to create a logical story.

Common Core State Standard used: W.K.5: With guidance and support from adults, respond to questions and suggestions from peers and add details to strengthen writing as needed.

Materials Needed:

Chart paper

Marker

Time for lesson: 15-30 minutes

Lesson (Small groups are best)

- Explain to students that sometimes we need to work together to get the best product possible, even with writing
- Tell students that you are going to start a story and then they are going to add to it one sentence at a time, until the story is complete.
- As the story is told, write it out on chart paper.

Assessment: Participation with appropriate input

W.K.5: Lesson Two

Title: I'm Going to Need More Detail

Topic: Strengthening writing with illustrations

Objective of lesson: Students will work together to create a logical illustration with a given sentence.

Common Core State Standard used: W.K.5: With guidance and support from adults, respond to questions and suggestions from peers and add details to strengthen writing as needed.

Materials Needed:

Paper

Pencil

Crayons

List of sentences (Samples included)

Time for lesson: 10-15 minutes

Lesson

- Tell students that sometimes we need help and that is ok. This includes different parts of writing, even the illustrations.

- Hand each student a sentence (included), making sure that each sentence is given to at least two students.

- Have students copy the sentence onto their individual papers. Read sentences to students if necessary.

- Have students draw a picture to go with their sentence.

- Next, have students trade with someone else with the same sentence. Allow that person to add details to the drawing and check spelling in the sentence. Offering corrections as needed.

Assessment: Participation with appropriate input or corrections

Sample sentences:

The dog jumped over a log in the park.

The cat ran away from the car.

The bear hid in the cave by the road.

The bug crawled up the stem of the flower.

The kids played in the park.

The bird had a nest in the tree.

The dog barked at the cat walking by.

The deer jumped into the woods.

The turtle crawled across the road.

The bug was lying in the floor.

W.K.6: Lesson One

Title: Paint Me Some Pictures

Topic: Using technology

Objective of lesson: Students will create pictures and labels using technology.

Common Core State Standard used: W.K.6: With guidance and support from adults, explore a variety of digital tools to produce and publish writing, including in collaboration with peers.

Materials Needed:

Computers (w/touch screen if possible)

Printer

Time for lesson: 20-30 minutes

Lesson

- This is a lesson for after students have been introduced to the Paintbrush program.

- Tell students that they get to be creative today and draw whatever they want as long as it is school appropriate.

- Have students draw at least five small pictures and label each with a one word description that they type without help.

Assessment: Participation

W.K.6: Lesson Two

Title: What's in a Name?

Topic: Using technology

Objective of lesson: Students will create a name board using interactive tools.

Common Core State Standard used: W.K .6: With guidance and support from adults, explore a variety of digital tools to produce and publish writing, including in collaboration with peers.

Materials Needed:

White interactive board

Time for lesson: 10-15 minutes

Lesson

- The goal is to have students use technology, so make it fun before using it for a more structured lesson.

- Set up the interactive white board and show students how to change the colors and use the pen.

- Allow students to go one at a time to write their names in any style they want on the board.

- Take pictures or screen grabs of the board to post. (This activity can be completed one at a time throughout the day.)

Assessment: Participation with correct usage of technology.

W.K.7: Lesson One

Title: I Think...

Topic: Sharing opinions on a selected set of books in a group

Objective of lesson: Students will share an opinion about a series or selection of books.

Common Core State Standard used: W.K.7: Participate in shared research and writing projects (e.g., explore a number of books by a favorite author and express opinions about them).

Materials Needed:

Selection of books from a series or same genre (Fairy tales, poems, fables, etc)

Time for lesson: 10-15 minutes (per day)

Lesson

- Read a short book or story from the genre or series each day.
- At the end of the week display all books for students to see and spend a few minutes discussing each.
- Ask students which book they liked best and why.

Assessment: Participation

W.K.7: Lesson Two

Title: Art Explosion

Topic: Sharing opinions in a group setting

Objective of lesson: Students will share an opinion about artwork

Common Core State Standard used: W.K .7: Participate in shared research and writing projects (e.g., explore a number of books by a favorite author and express opinions about them).

Materials Needed:

Selection of art prints from different artists

Time for lesson: 10-15 minutes

Lesson

- Allow students to view the artwork that is displayed around the room.
- Have students come together to discuss their opinions of the artwork.

Assessment: Participation

W.K.8: Lesson One

Title: Tell Me About A Time When...

Topic: Sharing personal experiences

Objective of lesson: Students will share a personal experience with the group.

Common Core State Standard used: W.K.8: With guidance and support from adults, recall information from experiences or gather information from provided sources to answer a question.

Materials Needed:

Text: *Today I Feel Silly and Other Moods* by Jamie Lee Curtis

Time for lesson: 10-30 minutes

Lesson

- Read the text to the class as a whole.
- Randomly choose a mood from the book.
- Ask a child to share a time that they felt (mood).

Assessment: Participation

W.K.8: Lesson Two

Title: What Did You Have?

Topic: Sharing personal experiences

Objective of lesson: Students will share a personal experience with the group.

Common Core State Standard used: W.K.8: With guidance and support from adults, recall information from experiences or gather information from provided sources to answer a question.

Materials Needed:

Paper

Crayons

Time for lesson: 10-30 minutes

Lesson

- Have students draw a picture of what they did the night before.
- One by one or in small groups have students share about the picture. (Small groups are best for shy children.)

Assessment: Participation

SL.K.1: Lesson One

Title: Rules of the Talk

Topic: Realizing the rules of conversation

Objective of lesson: Students will help write the rules of discussion.

Common Core State Standard used: SL.K.1: Participate in collaborative conversations with diverse partners about kindergarten topics and texts with peers and adults in small and larger groups.

Follow agreed-upon rules for discussions (e.g., listening to others and taking turns speaking about the topics and texts under discussion).

Continue a conversation through multiple exchanges.

Materials Needed:

Chart Paper

Markers

Time for lesson: 5-10 minutes

Lesson

- Have students discuss how best to talk with someone.
- Record and then post rules as a reminder of what students decided.

Assessment: Participation

SL.K.1: Lesson Two

Title: Talk About It

Topic: Realizing the rules of conversation

Objective of lesson: Students will practice discussing a topic with one another.

Common Core State Standard used: SL.K.1: Participate in collaborative conversations with diverse partners about kindergarten topics and texts with peers and adults in small and larger groups.

Follow agreed-upon rules for discussions (e.g., listening to others and taking turns speaking about the topics and texts under discussion).

Continue a conversation through multiple exchanges.

Materials Needed:

Timer

Time for lesson: 5 minutes

Lesson

- Pair students with someone they do not normally speak with in class (or use another kindergarten class if available)
- Set a timer so that students have five minutes to find out three things about each other (Full name, favorite thing to do, and favorite color)
- Allow students to introduce each other. Rules of discussion have to be followed to gain this information.

Assessment: Explain other person

Kindergarten

SL.K.2: Lesson One

Title: Recycle This

Topic: Answering questions

Objective of lesson: Students will demonstrate understanding on a story through demonstration.

Common Core State Standard used: SL.K.2: Confirm understanding of a text read aloud or information presented orally or through other media by asking and answering questions about key details and requesting clarification if something is not understood.

Materials Needed:

Text: *The Magic School Bus Gets Recycled* by Anne Capeci

Recyclables and bins

Time for lesson: 15 minutes

Lesson

- Read the text to children and spend time discussing the different types of recyclables.

- Split students into equal teams (5-7 children per team depending on class size.)

- Explain that they are going to sort the pile of recyclables you have into the correct bins, but they must work together as a team. (Have bins be different colors or have them labeled with pictures: colored plastic, clear plastic, paper)

- Allow each team to sort the recyclables, first finished and correctly sorted wins.

Assessment: Participation with accuracy

SL.K.2: Lesson Two

Title: Make It a Game

Topic: Answering questions

Objective of lesson: Students will answer basic questions about a text in small groups

Common Core State Standard used: SL.K.2: Confirm understanding of a text read aloud or information presented orally or through other media by asking and answering questions about key details and requesting clarification if something is not understood.

Materials Needed:

Text: *A Chair for My Mother* by Vera B. Williams

Bells or buzzers (one per child)

Time for lesson: 15 minutes (per group)

Lesson

- Read the text to students in a small group (ability groups are best for this activity)
- After reading, offer students a bell or buzzer. As each question is asked, have students ring in with the answer.

Assessment: Participation and correct answers

SL.K.3: Lesson One

Title: What Do You Do?

Topic: Asking questions

Objective of lesson: Students will interview their parents to gain new information.

Common Core State Standard used: SL.K.3: Ask and answer questions in order to seek help, get information, or clarity something that is not understood.

Materials Needed:

Video: http://www.youtube.com/watch?v=UZHSDjtD-dg

Time for lesson: 25 minutes for video + time for home interview

Lesson

- Allow students to watch the YouTube video about an interview with Elmo.

- After the video have students work together to come up with at least three questions for parents (other adult) to answer that night as an interview.

- Share answers the next day.

Assessment: Participation

SL.K.3: Lesson Two

Title: Answer Me This

Topic: Asking questions

Objective of lesson: Students will interview their teacher

Common Core State Standard used: SL.K.3: Ask and answer questions in order to seek help, get information, or clarify something that is not understood.

Materials Needed:

Room for a group to gather

Time for lesson: 10-15 minutes

Lesson

- Explain to students that as the teacher you know lots of information about them, but they may not know much about you.

- Allow each student to ask one unique question of you and answer appropriately.

Assessment: Participation

SL.K.4: Lesson One

Title: My Bedroom

Topic: Describing familiar places or things

Objective of lesson: Students will draw and describe their bedroom.

Common Core State Standard used: SL.K .4: Describe familiar people, places, things, and events and, with prompting and support, provide additional detail.

Materials Needed:

Paper

Crayons

Time for lesson: 10 minutes

Lesson

- Tell students that sometimes it is very important to know exactly where something is or how to get to a specific place, especially if you are lost or if something we love is lost.
- Have students draw their bedroom exactly as it is with all the small details, including toys, closet, bed, windows, and even outlets.

Assessment: Participation and appropriate drawing

SL.K.4: Lesson Two

Title: Fire Escape

Topic: Describing familiar places or things

Objective of lesson: Students will draw and describe an escape route in the school.

Common Core State Standard used: SL.K .4: Describe familiar people, places, things, and events and, with prompting and support, provide additional detail.

Materials Needed:

School outline with exits marked

Crayons

Time for lesson: 10-15 minutes

Lesson (Great during fire safety week)

- Explain to students that if an emergency, like a fire, would happen that they need to remain calm and know how to get out of the building.
- Have students work together to plan at least two escape routes from the school.
- Have students practice if possible.
- Have students do a home escape route with parents as homework.

Assessment: Participation and appropriate drawing

SL.K.5: Lesson One

Title: Finish This Drawing

Topic: Adding details

Objective of lesson: Students will add details to unfinished pictures.

Common Core State Standard used: SL.K.5: Add drawings or other visual displays to descriptions as desired to provide additional detail.

Materials Needed:

Outlines (Samples provided)

Crayons

Time for lesson: 10-30 minutes

Lesson

- Tell students that there are times, especially in reading and writing, that more detail is needed. This is also true of illustrations. Details are important.

- Allow students to see the outlines provided. Have students guess what the outline is of based on shape.

- Ask students what is missing and what needs to be added to complete the drawing.

- Allow students to finish each drawing. Prompt for detail around the animals.

Assessment: Detailed drawings.

Kindergarten 114

SL.K.5: Lesson Two

Title: Add To Me

Topic: Adding details

Objective of lesson: Students will add detail words to sentences then draw accompanying Illustrations

Common Core State Standard used: SL.K .5: Add drawings or other visual displays to descriptions as desired to provide additional detail.

Materials Needed:

Chart paper (To record new sentences)

Sentences (Samples included)

Paper

Crayons

Time for lesson: 10-30 minutes

Lesson

- Explain to students that details are important in reading and writing. Read a sample sentence to students: The dog jumped.

- Ask students how you could give more detail in the sentence: The big dog jumped the brown log (ex.) Prompt for answers.

- Now try a few more sample sentences.

- Have students draw detailed pictures of the sentences they have helped create.

Assessment: Detailed drawings and additions to sentences.

Sample Sentences:

The dog jumped.

The cat fell.

The tree grew.

The lamb lay.

The child sat.

The bird flew.

The woman listened.

My ears rang.

I dreamed.

The blanket was packed.

SL.K.6: Lesson One

Title: Pledge

Topic: Public Speaking

Objective of lesson: Students will speak audibly

Common Core State Standard used: SL.K.6: Speak audibly and express thoughts, feelings, and ideas clearly.

Materials Needed:

Flag

Time for lesson: 2 minutes

Lesson

- Choose a daily leader to begin saying the pledge to the flag for the class, allowing the class to join in.

Assessment: Clarity of speech

Kindergarten

SL.K.6: Lesson Two

Title: Something Special

Topic: Public Speaking

Objective of lesson: Students will speak audibly

Common Core State Standard used: SL.K.6: Speak audibly and express thoughts, feelings, and ideas clearly.

Materials Needed:

Time for lesson: 5-10 minutes

Lesson

- Each morning choose one or two children to share something special about the day before with the class. Make sure everyone gets a chance throughout the week.

Assessment: Clarity of speech

L.K.1: Lesson One

Title: Written Pairs

Topic: Upper and lower case letters

Objective of lesson: Students will practice writing upper and lower case letters

Common Core State Standard used: L.K.1: Demonstrate command of the conventions of standard English grammar and usage when writing or speaking.

Print many upper- and lowercase letters.

Use frequently occurring nouns and verbs.

Form regular plural nouns orally by adding /s/ or /es/ (e.g., dog, dogs; wish, wishes).

Understand and use question words (interrogatives) (e.g., who, what, where, when, why, how).

Use the most frequently occurring prepositions (e.g., to, from, in, out, on, off, for, of, by, with).

Produce and expand complete sentences in shared language activities.

Materials Needed:

Shaving Cream (Unscented)

Towels for cleanup

Time for lesson: 10-30 minutes

Lesson

- Tell students you are going to practice making letters, both upper and lower case.

- Explain the rules of shaving cream: None in the eyes, hands to yourself, must first do the letters as told, and then a little drawing on your own can happen.

- Spray shaving cream in front of each child or along a large table.

- Call out letters, both upper and lower cases to have students 'write' in shaving cream.

Assessment: Correct letter making, both upper and lowercase

L.K.1: Lesson Two

Title: Interrogation

Topic: Interrogatives

Objective of lesson: Students will practice using interrogatives

Common Core State Standard used: L.K .1: Demonstrate command of the conventions of standard English grammar and usage when writing or speaking.

Print many upper- and lowercase letters.

Use frequently occurring nouns and verbs.

Form regular plural nouns orally by adding /s/ or /es/ (e.g., dog, dogs; wish, wishes).

Understand and use question words (interrogatives) (e.g., who, what, where, when, why, how).

Use the most frequently occurring prepositions (e.g., to, from, in, out, on, off, for, of, by, with).

Produce and expand complete sentences in shared language activities.

Materials Needed:

Sentence strips

Interrogatives (Included)

Time for Lesson: 5-10 minutes

Kindergarten

Lesson

- Have sentence strips with partial questions written on them, but a blank where the interrogative would be: ___ will be at the party?; ___ long do we have to wait?; ___ did you put the book?

- Review the following words: who, what, when, where, why, how

- Place one sentence on the board or place all sentences around the room.

- Read the sentence as it is written and ask students who has a word that would be appropriate to fill in the blank.

Assessment: Correct answers

Who
What
Where
When
Why
How

L.K.2: Lesson One

Title: Name This

Topic: Punctuation

Objective of lesson: Students will practice identifying punctuation

Common Core State Standard used: L.K .2: Demonstrate command of the conventions of standard English capitalization, punctuation, and spelling when writing.

Capitalize the first word in a sentence and the pronoun I.

Recognize and name end punctuation.

Write a letter or letters for most consonant and short-vowel sounds (phonemes).

Materials Needed:

Chalk or white board

Chalk, marker, or digital pen

Time for Lesson: 5-10 minutes

Lesson

- Have several short sentences written on the board, each with different punctuation. (Period, question mark, exclamation point)
- Read each sentence in the manner it was written and have students identify the ending.

Assessment: Correct answers

L.K.2: Lesson Two

Title: Correct This

Topic: Command of the English language

Objective of lesson: Students will practice corrections

Common Core State Standard used: L.K .2: Demonstrate command of the conventions of standard English capitalization, punctuation, and spelling when writing.

Capitalize the first word in a sentence and the pronoun I.

Recognize and name end punctuation.

Write a letter or letters for most consonant and short-vowel sounds (phonemes).

Materials Needed:

Chalk or white board

Chalk, marker, or digital pen

Time for Lesson: 10-20 minutes

Lesson

- Place a sentence on the board and allow students one at a time to come up and make one correction each.
- Change sentences as needed. (If using an interactive white board, pressing the cheer button is an excellent motivator.)

Assessment: Correct answers

L.K.4: Lesson One

Title: Duck or Duck

Topic: Multiple meanings

Objective of lesson: Students will represent multiple meaning words.

Common Core State Standard used: L.K.4: Determine or clarify the meaning of unknown and multiple-meaning words and phrases based on kindergarten reading and content.

Identify new meanings for familiar words and apply them accurately (e.g., knowing duck is a bird and learning the verb to duck).

Use the most frequently occurring inflections and affixes (e.g., -ed, -s, re-, un-, pre-, -ful, -less) as a clue to the meaning of an unknown word.

Materials Needed:

List of multiple meaning words (Included)

Crayons

Paper

Glue

Magazines

Scissors

Time for Lesson: 10-30 minutes

Kindergarten

Lesson

- Show students the list of multiple meaning words.

- Choose one word to demonstrate for students, such as duck. (Bending to avoid something or an animal that quacks)

- Have students find or draw pictures to represent both meanings of a set number of words. Place meanings on paper side by side with the single multiple meaning word written above. (See Sample)

Assessment: Correct representations

Duck (animal)   Duck (hide, protect head)

Multiple Meaning Words:

Duck	Bat	Fly
Jar	Block	Foot
Back	Box	Ring
Bark	Date	Watch
Bill	Fall	Wave

L.K.4: Lesson Two

Title: A Wave to You?

Topic: Multiple meanings

Objective of lesson: Students will recognize multiple meaning words.

Common Core State Standard used: L.K .4: Determine or clarify the meaning of unknown and multiple-meaning words and phrases based on kindergarten reading and content.

Identify new meanings for familiar words and apply them accurately (e.g., knowing duck is a bird and learning the verb to duck).

Use the most frequently occurring inflections and affixes (e.g., -ed, -s, re-, un-, pre-, -ful, -less) as a clue to the meaning of an unknown word.

Materials Needed:

List of multiple meaning words and pictures (Included)

Time for Lesson: 10-30 minutes

Lesson

- Show students the list of multiple meaning words.
- Read a sentence using one of the multiple meaning words and allow students to point to a picture of which meaning is used in the sentence. (Ex. A duck flew by the window or I had to duck to avoid being hit)
- Repeat with numerous words so each child can participate.

Assessment: Correct representations

Kindergarten

Duck

Bat

Fly

Jar

Block

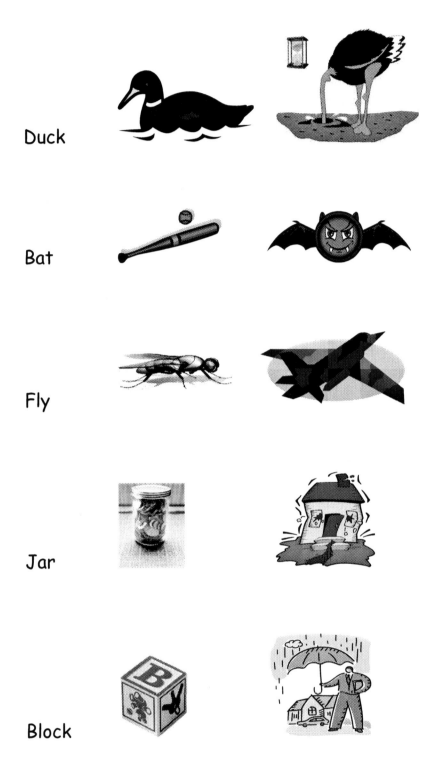

Kindergarten

Foot

Back

Box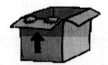

Ring

Bark

Kindergarten

Date

Watch

Bill

Fall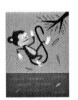

Wave

L.K.5: Lesson One

Title: Opposite Of

Topic: Antonyms

Objective of lesson: Students will demonstrate the opposite of high frequency verbs

Common Core State Standard used: L.K .5: With guidance and support from adults, explore word relationships and nuances in word meanings.

Sort common objects into categories (e.g., shapes, foods) to gain a sense of the concepts the categories represent.

Demonstrate understanding of frequently occurring verbs and adjectives by relating them to their opposites (antonyms).

Identify real-life connections between words and their use (e.g., note places at school that are colorful).

Distinguish shades of meaning among verbs describing the same general action (e.g., walk, march, strut, prance) by acting out the meanings.

Materials Needed:

List of high frequency words and antonyms

Time for Lesson: 5-10 minutes

Lesson

- Have students stand in an area that gives them room to move.

Kindergarten

- Explain that you are going to say a word or phrase and they are going to demonstrate the opposite. So if you say stand, they will sit, etc.
- Continue through several verbs. (This is great when students are restless)

Assessment: Participation

Word List:

Run (Walk)

Stand (Sit)

Up (Down)

Smile (Frown)

Moving (Still)

Carry (Drop)

Float (Fall)

Loud (Silent)

Moving (Still)

Healthy (Sick)

L.K.5: Lesson Two

Title: Sort It Out

Topic: Sorting

Objective of lesson: Students will categorize

Common Core State Standard used: L.K.5: With guidance and support from adults, explore word relationships and nuances in word meanings.

Sort common objects into categories (e.g., shapes, foods) to gain a sense of the concepts the categories represent.

Demonstrate understanding of frequently occurring verbs and adjectives by relating them to their opposites (antonyms).

Identify real-life connections between words and their use (e.g., note places at school that are colorful).

Distinguish shades of meaning among verbs describing the same general action (e.g., walk, march, strut, prance) by acting out the meanings.

Materials Needed:

Objects that can be sorted by color, shape, or group (animal, food, plant)

Time for Lesson: 10-15 minutes

Lesson (Small groups)

- Provide each small group with a selection of items.

- Tell each group they have 1 minute to sort all items into sensible groups

Kindergarten

- Switch groups and items after checking for accuracy and mixing items back up.

Assessment: Participation and correct sorting

K.CC.1: Lesson One

Title: Count On Me

Topic: Counting to 100

Objective of lesson: Students will count to 100

Common Core State Standard used: K.CC.1: Count to 100 by ones and by tens

Materials Needed:

100 candies for each student (M&M's, Skittles, and Nerds work best)

Time for Lesson: 5-10 minutes

Lesson

- Tell students that you are going to have a very tasty math lesson, but if they eat before they count, all candies go in the trash.

- Have students count 1 at a time how many M&M's they have. Have students to make a mark on a paper or groups sets of ten.

Assessment: Counting and grouping

K.CC.1: Lesson Two

Title: 100's Day

Topic: Counting to 100

Objective of lesson: Students will count to 100

Common Core State Standard used: K.CC.1: Count to 100 by ones and by tens

Materials Needed:

Student brings material

Time for Lesson: 10-15 minutes

Lesson

- The night before this lesson (100th day of school is great) have students ask parents for 100 of something.

- Allow students to share their '100' with the class and then count to make sure the number is correct.

- Have students group 10 items per group for easy checking.

Assessment: Counting and grouping

K.CC.2: Lesson One

Title: You Can Count On Me

Topic: Counting forward in a known sequence

Objective of lesson: Students will count beginning with numbers other than one

Common Core State Standard used: K.CC.2: Count forward beginning from a given number within the known sequence (instead of having to begin at 1).

Materials Needed:

Name tags or sticky notes

Time for Lesson: 10-20 minutes

Lesson

- Give each student a tag with a different number on it…2-25 (or number of students in class) Do not use 1

- Choose random students and tell them, starting with their number, put people in order after them. May want to give the teacher and/or aide the highest numbers so everyone will have at least one person to put in order.

Assessment: Correct ordering

K.CC.2: Lesson Two

Title: Count It Up

Topic: Counting forward in a known sequence

Objective of lesson: Students will count beginning with numbers other than one

Common Core State Standard used: K.CC.2: Count forward beginning from a given number within the known sequence (instead of having to begin at 1).

Materials Needed:

Number tiles (set for each student, 1-20)

Time for Lesson: 10-15 minutes

Lesson

- Have students lay number tiles right side up.
- Say a number and have students place that time in front of them and put other tiles in order.
- Check each sequence.

Assessment: Correct sequencing

K.CC.3: Lesson One

Title: Taking the Test

Topic: Writing numbers 0-20

Objective of lesson: Students will write numbers 0-20

Common Core State Standard used: K.CC.3: Write numbers from 0 to 20. Represent a number of objects with a written numeral 0-20 (with 0 representing a count of no objects).

Materials Needed:

Paper

Pencil

Time for Lesson: 5-10 minutes

Lesson

- Tell students you are going to take a quick test.
- Have students number 0-20, because this is a special test.
- Have students hand in the test ☺

Assessment: Correct writing of numbers

K.CC.3: Lesson Two

Title: Write and Wipe

Topic: Writing numbers 0-20

Objective of lesson: Students will count beginning with numbers other than one

Common Core State Standard used: K.CC.3: Write numbers from 0 to 20. Represent a number of objects with a written numeral 0-20 (with 0 representing a count of no objects).

Materials Needed:

Mini dry erase boards or homemade ones (Card stock in a sheet protector)

Dry erase markers

Paper towels (erasers)

Time for Lesson: 5-10 minutes

Lesson

- Have students write the numbers 0-20 as you call them out in random order.

- After each number is written have students hold it up for easy checking and then erase before the next number.

Assessment: Correct writing of numbers

K.CC.4: Lesson One

Title: One on One

Topic: Counting and cardinality

Objective of lesson: Students will pair objects one to one with counting

Common Core State Standard used: K.CC.4: Understand the relationship between numbers and quantities; connect counting to cardinality.

When counting objects, say the number names in the standard order, pairing each object with one and only one number name and each number name with one and only one object.

Understand that the last number name said tells the number of objects counted. The number of objects is the same regardless of their arrangement or the order in which they were counted.

Understand that each successive number name refers to a quantity that is one larger.

Materials Needed:

Blocks or tiles

Time for Lesson: 5-10 minutes

Lesson

- Offer a selection of blocks or tiles to each student
- Ask students to demonstrate counting by saying a number of particular types of blocks (3 green blocks or 5 triangles).

- Repeat with various numbers.

Assessment: Correct one to one ratio creation

K.CC.4: Lesson Two

Title: How Many

Topic: Counting and cardinality

Objective of lesson: Students will pair objects one to one with counting and identify final amounts

Common Core State Standard used: K.CC.4: Understand the relationship between numbers and quantities; connect counting to cardinality.

When counting objects, say the number names in the standard order, pairing each object with one and only one number name and each number name with one and only one object.

Understand that the last number name said tells the number of objects counted. The number of objects is the same regardless of their arrangement or the order in which they were counted.

Understand that each successive number name refers to a quantity that is one larger.

Materials Needed:

Markers

Time for Lesson: 5-10 minutes

Lesson

- Have students gather in an area in which they can see the board or large chart paper.
- Draw a number of shapes or marks and have students count.

- Ask students how many were counted. Now ask how many are total.

Remind students that the last number they say is the same as the total there if they have counted correctly.

Assessment: Participation.

K.CC.5: Lesson One

Title: Count Me Out

Topic: Counting unusually arranged items correctly

Objective of lesson: Students will correctly count items that have been arranged in a specific style.

Common Core State Standard used: K.CC.5: Count to answer "how many?" questions about as many as 20 things arranged in a line, a rectangular array, or a circle, or as many as 10 things in a scattered configuration; given a number from 1-20, count out that many objects.

Materials Needed:

Magnets

Magnetic board

Time for Lesson: 5-10 minutes

Lesson

- Have students sit where they can easily see magnets and board.
- Arrange magnets in different orders with different numbers of magnets and have students count them out.

Assessment: Participation and correct counting

K.CC.5: Lesson Two

Title: Mark It Out

Topic: Counting unusually arranged items correctly

Objective of lesson: Students will correctly count items that have been arranged in a specific style.

Common Core State Standard used: K.CC.5: Count to answer "how many?" questions about as many as 20 things arranged in a line, a rectangular array, or a circle, or as many as 10 things in a scattered configuration; given a number from 1-20, count out that many objects.

Materials Needed:

Worksheet (Included)

Time for Lesson: 5-10 minutes

Lesson

- Before handing out worksheets, demonstrate how to mark out a picture after it has been counted.
- Hand out worksheets and allow students to count.

Assessment: Correct counting

Kindergarten   148

How many are in each group?

1. _____   2. _____

   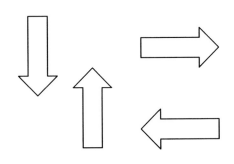

3. _____   4. _____

5. _____   6. _____

K.CC.6: Lesson One

Title: Are There More?

Topic: Greater than or less than

Objective of lesson: Students will identify greater than and less than

Common Core State Standard used: K.CC.6: Identify whether the number of objects in one group is greater than, less than, or equal to the number of objects in another group, e.g., by using matching and counting strategies.

Materials Needed:

Selection of objects in different sizes (Beads are great)

Time for Lesson: 10-15 minutes

Lesson (Small groups)

- Gather students in groups of 4-5 for this lesson.

- Set out different sized beads.

- Place a set number of beads in two piles and ask which pile has the most beads.

- Continue through several sets, each time asking which pile has the most or the biggest number. Make sure to have at least one or two piles in which the biggest beads are actually in the pile with the lowest number.

Assessment: Correct identification of the larger number of objects

K.CC.6: Lesson Two

Title: Make This Bigger

Topic: Greater than or less than

Objective of lesson: Students will identify greater than and less than

Common Core State Standard used: K.CC.6: Identify whether the number of objects in one group is greater than, less than, or equal to the number of objects in another group, e.g., by using matching and counting strategies.

Materials Needed:

Selection of objects in different sizes (Beads are great)

Overhead

Time for Lesson: 10-15 minutes

Lesson

- Have a pile of beads or blocks ready beside the overhead.
- Call students up one at a time and ask them to make different combinations (Make a row that is one bigger than the other, make two equal rows of beads, Make a row of beads that is one less than the other)
- Allow all students to try one or two items then have other students decide whether or not it is correct.

Assessment: Making groups smaller, larger, or equal

K.CC.7: Lesson One

Title: Feed The Mathigator

Topic: Greater than or less than

Objective of lesson: Students will identify greater than and less than

Common Core State Standard used: K.CC.7: Compare two numbers between 1 and 10 presented as written numerals.

Materials Needed:

Mathigator Puppet (Included, will need glue, paper bag, and scissors)

Number tiles (Included)

Time for Lesson: 10-30 minutes (For construction of the mathigator)

Lesson

- Explain to students that mathigators are very hungry creatures and they only eat the largest numbers available.
- Tell students to pull two numbers from their number line. (Your choice)
- Have students feed the mathigator the largest of the two numbers.

Assessment: Correct identification of larger numbers

1	2	3	4	5
6	7	8	9	10

Kindergarten

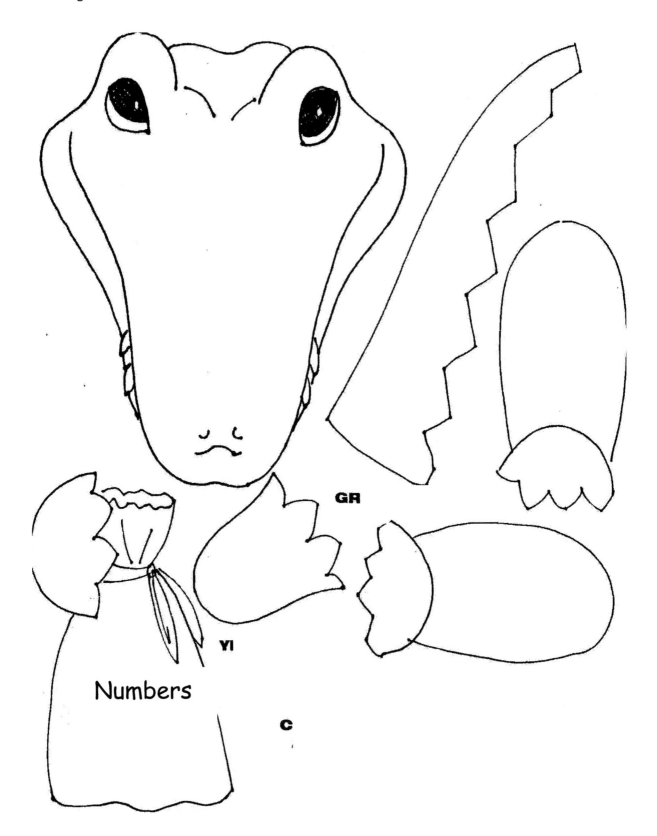

K.CC.7: Lesson Two

Title: Point Me in the Right Direction

Topic: Greater than or less than

Objective of lesson: Students will identify greater than and less than

Common Core State Standard used: K.CC.7: Compare two numbers between 1 and 10 presented as written numerals.

Materials Needed:

Mathigator (Directions included)

Green paint or markers

Clothespin (pinch kind) for each child

Wiggly eyes (Optional)

Time for Lesson: 10-30 minutes (For construction of the mathigator)

Lesson

- Have students paint the clothespin green all over. After drying, students can add eyes or draw on eyes on the end that would normally be pinched. (This looks like an open mouth)

- Explain that mathigators always attack big numbers with an open mouth. Write two numbers on the board and have students point their mathigators toward the largest number.

- Repeat with various numbers.

Assessment: Correct identification of larger numbers

K.OA.1: Lesson One

Title: Stomp It Out

Topic: Addition with movement

Objective of lesson: Students will add two numbers that are equal to or less than 10

Common Core State Standard used: K.OA:1: Represent addition and subtraction with objects, fingers, mental images, drawings, sounds (e.g., claps), acting out situations, verbal explanations, expressions, or equations

Materials Needed:

Board or whiteboard to write problems

Plenty of space

Time for Lesson: 5-10 minutes

Lesson

- Have several problems written on the board, but covered until time to use them.
- Tell students that they are going to do math and get some exercise today.
- Have students stand and stomp out the first number with their right foot, the second number with the left foot, and then add those numbers and stomp the total by jumping with both feet.

Assessment: Correct addition

K.OA.1: Lesson Two

Title: Magic Math

Topic: Subtraction

Objective of lesson: Students will subtract two numbers that are equal to or less than 10

Common Core State Standard used: K.OA:1: Represent addition and subtraction with objects, fingers, mental images, drawings, sounds (e.g., claps), acting out situations, verbal explanations, expressions, or equations

Materials Needed:

Magic wand (For teacher or leader only)

Time for Lesson: 5-10 minutes

Lesson

- Tell students that math can make magic. Demonstrate with the following trick: Hold up both hands, tell students that you have 6 fingers on one hand, count all your fingers out loud. Now count your fingers backwards from 10. Your first hand will end on six. See 6 fingers on one hand☺!

- Now that students are interested, tell them that you are going to do math magic today. Write a simple problem on the board. Have students hold up however many fingers to represent the larger number.

- Now wave your magic wand and as you do, tell students that the second number in the problem of fingers will fold down.
- Explain that the magic is that the number of fingers left up is the answer to the problem on the board.

Assessment: Correct subtraction

K.OA.2: Lesson One

Title: Draw It Out

Topic: Word problems

Objective of lesson: Students will complete addition word problems through illustrations.

Common Core State Standard used: K.OA:2: Solve addition and subtraction word problems, and add and subtract within 10, e.g., by using objects or drawings to represent the problem.

Materials Needed:

Word problems (Samples included)

Crayons

Paper

Time for Lesson: 10-20 minutes

Lesson

- Demonstrate for students how to solve a word problem by looking for key words and drawing pictures.
- Have students draw pictures to help them solve written word problems you share.

Assessment: Correct addition and illustrations

Kindergarten

Sample Problems:

Anna had 3 apples. George bought 2 more apples to give to Anna. How many apples will Anna have now?

The teacher was being nice and giving out stickers. She gave two stickers to Sarah. She then gave five stickers to Ben. How many stickers did the teacher give out?

We decided to build a house out of popsicle sticks. We started by building two sides with five sticks each. How many total sticks were used to make the two sides?

There were two horses standing in a field. Each horse had four legs. How many legs were there total?

Sandy and Angie share a birthday. I needed to buy gifts for both girls. I bought Sandy 2 gifts and Angie four small gifts. How many gifts did I buy?

We had a picnic outside. I watched as 8 little ants crawled toward the food. Then two more ants came crawling forward. How many ants were at the picnic?

K.OA.2: Lesson Two

Title: Show Me How It Goes

Topic: Subtraction

Objective of lesson: Students will complete subtraction word problems through demonstration.

Common Core State Standard used: K.OA:2: Solve addition and subtraction word problems, and add and subtract within 10, e.g., by using objects or drawings to represent the problem.

Materials Needed

Blocks for each child (At least 10)

Word problems (Samples included)

Time for Lesson: 10-20 minutes

Lesson

- Hand out ten blocks per student.
- Read each problem aloud and have students demonstrate how to solve by using their blocks. Remind students that the biggest number is what they will always start with in subtraction.

Assessment: Correct subtraction through demonstration

Kindergarten

Sample Problems:

Amy had 7 blocks on the table. Two blocks fell off the table. How many blocks were left on the table?

Benji had 5 blocks on his chair. He decided to put away 3 blocks. How many blocks does he have left?

Maurice had two blocks in front of him. Both were put away by his teacher. How many blocks were left?

All ten blocks had been stacked up on the desk. A younger students walked by and took 5 of the blocks. How many were left?

One block sat in the middle of the table. School ended and no one moved the block. How many blocks were in the middle of the table?

Eight blocks were stacked one on top of the other. Someone walked by and took the top three off the stack. How many were left?

K.OA.3: Lesson One

Title: And _____ Makes 10

Topic: Addition using manipulatives

Objective of lesson: Students will decompose numbers less than or equal to 10

Common Core State Standard used: K.OA:3: Decompose numbers less than or equal to 10 into pairs in more than one way, e.g., by using objects or drawings, and record each decomposition by a drawing or equation (e.g., 5 = 2 + 3 and 5 = 4 + 1).

Materials Needed

Blocks for each child (At least 20) or some other objects

Problems (Samples included)

Time for Lesson: 5-10 minutes

Lesson

- Show students a sample of how to fill in a missing number to make ten.
- Allow students to use manipulatives to make problems work out to 10.

Assessment: Correct addition to ten.

Sample Problems:

3 + ___ = 10

___ + 5 = 10

1 + ___ = 10

8 + ___ = 10

9 + ___ = 10

4 + ___ = 10

2 + ___ = 10

___ + 6 = 10

7 + ___ =10

0 + ___ = 10

K.OA.3: Lesson Two

Title: Slap Me Ten

Topic: Addition using playing cards

Objective of lesson: Students will make ten out of playing cards

Common Core State Standard used: K.OA:3: Decompose numbers less than or equal to 10 into pairs in more than one way, e.g., by using objects or drawings, and record each decomposition by a drawing or equation (e.g., 5 = 2 + 3 and 5 = 4 + 1).

Materials Needed

Playing cards with Face cards and Jokers removed (Aces will serve as ones)

Time for Lesson: 5-10 minutes

Lesson (Small groups)

- Deal out all cards in the deck to yourself and the students.
- Lay down a card and have students identify the number.
- Ask students who can find a card the fastest, that can be added to that card to make 10.

Assessment: Correct addition to ten.

K.OA.4: Lesson One

Title: Roll 'Em Up

Topic: Making ten

Objective of lesson: Students will make ten out of manipulatives

Common Core State Standard used: K.OA:4: For any number from 1 to 9, find the number that makes 10 when added to the given number, e.g., by using objects or drawings, and record the answer with a drawing or equation.

Materials Needed

Play dough

Time for Lesson: 10-15 minutes

Lesson (Small groups)

- Give each student some play dough.
- Make ten play dough balls and set in front of you, have students do the same.
- Now take away a given number (your choice) of balls and ask students how many you would need to make ten.
- Have students display that missing number in front of them.

Assessment: Correct addition to ten.

K.OA.4: Lesson Two

Title: Magnet Math

Topic: Making ten

Objective of lesson: Students will make ten out of magnetic numbers

Common Core State Standard used: K.OA:4: For any number from 1 to 9, find the number that makes 10 when added to the given number, e.g., by using objects or drawings, and record the answer with a drawing or equation.

Materials Needed

Magnetic numbers

Time for Lesson: 10-15 minutes

Lesson

- Tell students that they will be in charge of teaching the class today.

- Have students come to the board one at a time and create a math problem that equals 10 using the magnetic numbers.

Assessment: Correct addition to ten.

K.OA.5: Lesson One

Title: Minute Math Race

Topic: Subtracting under 5

Objective of lesson: Students will subtract within the number 5

Common Core State Standard used: K.OA:5: Fluently add and subtract within 5

Materials Needed

Minute Math Sheet (Included)

Timer

Time for Lesson: 5 minutes

Lesson

- Tell students that this is a math challenge.
- Hand out worksheets and set the timer.
- Tell students that the goal is to improve over time and get the answers right. Explain that when the timer starts they need to work as fast as possible.
- When the timer stops, pencils down, even if not finished.
- Allow students to record scores over time.

Assessment: Correct answers to subtraction problems, improvement over time

Minute Math

5 - 3 = _____

4 - 2 = _____

2 - 2 = _____

3 - 2 = _____

5 - 4 = _____

4 - 2 = _____

2 - 0 = _____

0 - 0 = _____

5 - 2 = _____

3 - 1 = _____

1 - 1 = _____

4 - 3 = _____

5 - 1 = _____

5 - 5 = _____

K.OA.5: Lesson Two

Title: Sweet Subtraction

Topic: Subtracting under 5

Objective of lesson: Students will subtract within the number 5

Common Core State Standard used: K.OA:5: Fluently add and subtract within 5

Materials Needed

Nerds candies for all students

Time for Lesson: 10-15 minutes

Lesson

- Give each student a pack of Nerds candy.
- Tell students that they will get to eat their lesson, but they must do it correctly.
- Have students lay out 5 nerds.
- Give students a math problem that is 5 minus (your choice).
- Allow students to eat the Nerds that you have asked to be subtracted.
- Ask how many Nerds are left.

Assessment: Correct answers to subtraction problems

K.NBT.1: Lesson One

Title: Pick Me, Pick Me

Topic: Ones and tens spots

Objective of lesson: Students will learn to add ones and tens to create numbers 11-19

Common Core State Standard used: K.NBT:1: Compose and decompose numbers from 11 to 19 into ten ones and some further ones, e.g., by using objects or drawings, and record each composition or decomposition by a drawing or equation (such as 18 = 10 + 8); understand that these numbers are composed of ten ones and one, two, three, four, five, six, seven, eight, or nine ones.

Materials Needed

Paper or Mini dry-erase boards

Time for Lesson: 10-15 minutes

Lesson

- Have a selection of students line up in the front of the room.

- Give each student a board or piece of paper. Each should contain a number 1-10 (one of each).

- The ten will always be part of the answer. Have the student holding the ten to step forward.

- Ask a student without a number how many ones would have to be added to make that ten a ex. 18 (The answer is 8).

- If the student is correct, they can replace one of the number holders that they used.
- Continue until everyone has had a chance to add ones to tens.

Assessment: Correct creation of a problem

K.NBT.1: Lesson Two

Title: Line It Up

Topic: Ones and tens spots

Objective of lesson: Students will learn to add ones and tens to create numbers 11-19

Common Core State Standard used: K.NBT:1: Compose and decompose numbers from 11 to 19 into ten ones and some further ones, e.g., by using objects or drawings, and record each composition or decomposition by a drawing or equation (such as 18 = 10 + 8); understand that these numbers are composed of ten ones and one, two, three, four, five, six, seven, eight, or nine ones.

Materials Needed

Board

Time for Lesson: 5 minutes

Lesson

- List several one and two digit numbers on the board.
- Draw a T-square and label ones and tens section.
- Have students write new numbers in and identify tens and ones columns.

Assessment: Participation and understanding

K.MD.1: Lesson One

Title: How Do I Measure Up?

Topic: Describing measureable attributes

Objective of lesson: Students will describe measureable attributes

Common Core State Standard used: K.MD:1: Describe measurable attributes of objects, such as length or weight. Describe several measurable attributes of a single object.

Materials Needed

Height chart to measure and record student heights

Time for Lesson: 10-15 minutes

Lesson

- Measure and record each student's height on a chart
- Have a select student look at the chart and ask a specific question of that student: Is Haley shorter or taller than Ben?
- Continue until everyone has answered a question.

Assessment: Participation

K.MD.1: Lesson Two

Title: Wait On The Weight

Topic: Describing measureable attributes

Objective of lesson: Students will describe measureable attributes

Common Core State Standard used: K.MD:1: Describe measurable attributes of objects, such as length or weight. Describe several measurable attributes of a single object.

Materials Needed

Scale

Selection of small objects

Time for Lesson: 10-15 minutes

Lesson

- Teach children to use a scale to measure and record object weights.

- Have children compare object size through specific questioning.

Assessment: Participation and comparison

K.MD.2: Lesson One

Title: String Theory

Topic: Comparing measureable attributes

Objective of lesson: Students will directly compare measureable attributes

Common Core State Standard used: K.MD:2: Directly compare two objects with a measurable attribute in common, to see which object has "more of"/"less of" the attribute, and describe the difference.

Materials Needed

Rulers

Several different lengths of string/yarn for each student

Time for Lesson: 5-10 minutes

Lesson

- Offer each student 3 to 5 different lengths of string
- Show students how to use a ruler to measure the length of the string pieces.
- Have students find different strings in their bunch :Show me your shortest string, Show me your longest string, place the longest and shortest string beside each other, etc.

Assessment: Participation and comparison

K.MD.2: Lesson Two

Title: Build Them Up or Down

Topic: Comparing measureable attributes

Objective of lesson: Students will directly compare measureable attributes

Common Core State Standard used: K.MD:2: Directly compare two objects with a measurable attribute in common, to see which object has "more of"/"less of" the attribute, and describe the difference.

Materials Needed

Wooden blocks

Time for Lesson: 5-10 minutes (Per questions: widest, tallest, thinnest)

Lesson

- Have several piles of blocks of the same number and shape lying in front of you.
- Show students how you can use the blocks to build different forms of different heights. (Use all blocks, but in different ways)
- Now let small groups of students try to build the widest or tallest building possible using the same number of blocks.
- Have students compare structures.

Assessment: Participation and comparison

K.MD.3: Lesson One

Title: Sort It Out

Topic: Sorting

Objective of lesson: Students will sort objects appropriately

Common Core State Standard used: K.MD:3: Classify objects into given categories; count the numbers of objects in each category and sort the categories by count

Materials Needed

Math shapes in a variety of colors

Time for Lesson: 5-10 minutes

Lesson

- Give students a selection of different size, color, and shaped math blocks.
- Have students separate blocks according to your direction.
- After one or two sorting, have students see if they can come up with a different way to sort.

Assessment: Correct sorting

K.MD.3: Lesson Two

Title: Kid Sort

Topic: Sorting

Objective of lesson: Students will sort each other appropriately

Common Core State Standard used: K.MD:3: Classify objects into given categories; count the numbers of objects in each category and sort the categories by count

Materials Needed

Students

Time for Lesson: 10-15 minutes

Lesson

- Tell students that they are going to find all different ways of sorting today, but they will not be sorting toys or blocks or shapes. They will sort themselves.

- Explain that together they are going to try to figure out ways to sort each other such as type of shoes, long or short hair, shirt color, etc.

- Proceed with sorts.

Assessment: Correct sorting and participation

K.G.1: Lesson One

Title: Find A Place

Topic: Placing objects in relation to one another

Objective of lesson: Students will appropriately place one object in relation to another

Common Core State Standard used: K.G:1: Describe objects in the environment using names of shapes, and describe the relative positions of these objects using terms such as above, below, beside, in front of, behind, and next to.

Materials Needed

Chairs (1 per student)

Blocks (1 per student)

Time for Lesson: 10-15 minutes

Lesson

- Give each student one block. Explain that you are going to see if they can follow directions.
- Start asking students to move the block in relation to the chair or other classroom objects.

Assessment: Correct placement

K.G.1: Lesson Two

Title: Where Is The...

Topic: Describing object placement

Objective of lesson: Students will appropriately describe the placement of an object

Common Core State Standard used: K.G:1: Describe objects in the environment using names of shapes, and describe the relative positions of these objects using terms such as above, below, beside, in front of, behind, and next to.

Materials Needed

Blocks

Time for Lesson: 5-10 minutes

Lesson

- Place several blocks of different colors around the classroom
- Ask one student at a time to describe the location of a certain block verbally. (Where is the green block: On top of the chair)
- Move blocks to offer new opportunities for every student.

Assessment: Correct description

K.G.2: Lesson One

Title: My Name Is....

Topic: Shapes

Objective of lesson: Students will appropriately name shapes

Common Core State Standard used: K.G:2: Correctly name shapes regardless of their orientations or overall size.

Materials Needed

Shape flash cards (Included)

Time for Lesson: 3 minutes (per child)

Lesson

- Use flash cards to individually quiz students on shapes.
- After flipping through the flash cards have students describe how they recognize at least one of the shapes. Such as a triangle has three sides or a circle has no corners.

Assessment: Correct identification

K.G.2: Lesson Two

Title: Shape Up

Topic: Shapes

Objective of lesson: Students will appropriately locate and name shapes

Common Core State Standard used: K.G:2: Correctly name shapes regardless of their orientations or overall size.

Materials Needed

Classroom or outdoor area

Time for Lesson: 5 minutes

Lesson

- Tell students you are going to go on a shape scavenger hunt. Tell them you will call out a shape and they are to raise their hand when they find something in the area that is that shape.
- Start saying shapes and allowing students to identify.

Assessment: Correct identification of shapes

Kindergarten

K.G.3: Lesson One

Title: Shape Flattering Design

Topic: Shapes

Objective of lesson: Students will appropriately identify shapes as flat or three dimensional

Common Core State Standard used: K.G:3: Identify shapes as two-dimensional (lying in a plane, "flat") or three-dimensional ("solid").

Materials Needed

Drawings of flat and three dimensional objects (Included)

Time for Lesson: 5 minutes

Lesson

- Show students flat shapes first and have them identify each shape.
- Next show students 3D shapes and help them identify the new names of these shapes (cube, sphere, pyramid, etc)
- Next have students identify the differences between the 3D and flat versions of the shapes.

Assessment: Correct identification of shapes as 3D or flat

Kindergarten

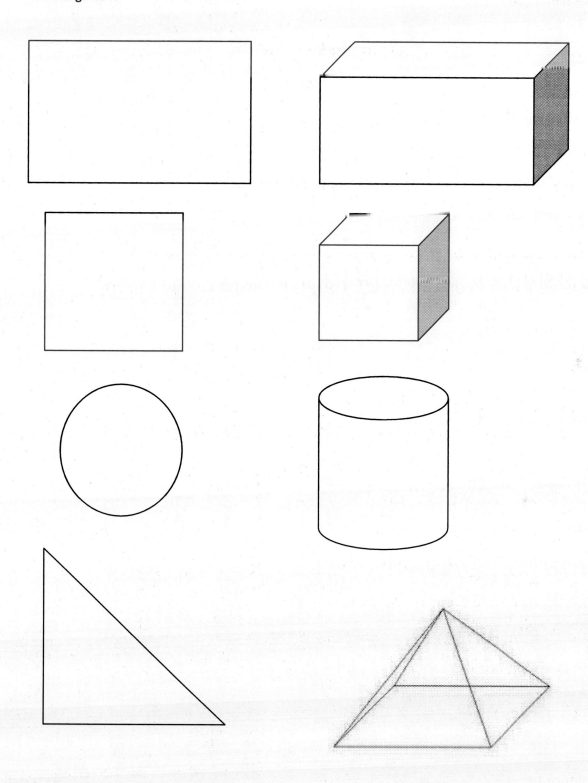

K.G.3: Lesson Two

Title: Flat or Full Figured

Topic: Shapes

Objective of lesson: Students will appropriately identify shapes as flat or three dimensional

Common Core State Standard used: K.G:3: Identify shapes as two-dimensional (lying in a plane, "flat") or three-dimensional ("solid").

Materials Needed

Shape cubes that are both flat and three dimensional

Time for Lesson: 5 minutes

Lesson

- Allow students to explore shapes, count sides, and pair flat with 3D if desired.
- Have students sort shapes into two baskets, flat or 3D

Assessment: Correct identification of shapes as 3D or flat

Kindergarten

K.G.4: Lesson One

Title: Talk About Shapely

Topic: Shapes

Objective of lesson: Students will describe shapes appropriately

Common Core State Standard used: K.G:4: Analyze and compare two- and three-dimensional shapes, in different sizes and orientations, using informal language to describe their similarities, differences, parts (e.g., number of sides and vertices/"corners") and other attributes (e.g., having sides of equal length).

Materials Needed

Shape cubes that are both flat and three dimensional

Time for Lesson: 5 minutes

Lesson

- Allow students to explore different flat and three dimensional objects.

- Ask specific questions about shapes to draw students' attention. (How many corners does the cube have? How about the flat square? How many flat squares would it take to make one cube?)

Assessment: Correct answering of questions about shapes

K.G.4: Lesson Two

Title: Draw It Up

Topic: Shapes

Objective of lesson: Students will practice drawing in 3D

Common Core State Standard used: K.G:4: Analyze and compare two- and three-dimensional shapes, in different sizes and orientations, using informal language to describe their similarities, differences, parts (e.g., number of sides and vertices/"corners") and other attributes (e.g., having sides of equal length).

Materials Needed

Sample drawing video (Link included)

Computer and projector

Time for Lesson: 10 minutes

Lesson

- To help students understand how to create flat vs. 3D shapes. Teach them to draw each shape using the video http://www.youtube.com/watch?v=C_88zW9MsbQ
- Allow students to practice

Assessment: Participation

K.G.5: Lesson One

Title: Model For Me

Topic: Making shapes

Objective of lesson: Students will create shapes

Common Core State Standard used: K.G:5: Model shapes in the world by building shapes from components (e.g., sticks and clay balls) and drawing shapes.

Materials Needed

Modeling clay

Time for Lesson: 10 minutes

Lesson

- Have photos of shapes available so students can review if necessary.

- Have students create the shapes as in the photos, paying special attention to number of sides, corners, or lack of corners

Assessment: Correct creation of shapes

K.G.5: Lesson Two

Title: Pick A Shape

Topic: Making shapes

Objective of lesson: Students will create shapes

Common Core State Standard used: K.G:5: Model shapes in the world by building shapes from components (e.g., sticks and clay balls) and drawing shapes.

Materials Needed

Popsicle sticks

Glue

Time for Lesson: 15 minutes

Lesson

- Provide plenty of glue and popsicle sticks for students.
- Have each student create the following shapes from popsicle sticks (Square, rectangle, triangle)
- Try two challenge shapes of a 3D cube and an octagon.

Assessment: Correct creation of shapes

K.G.6: Lesson One

Title: Two + Two = Square

Topic: Combining shapes into new shapes

Objective of lesson: Students will combine shapes to form new shapes

Common Core State Standard used: K.G:6: Compose simple shapes to form larger shapes

Materials Needed

Flat Math shapes of various sizes

Time for Lesson: 5-10 minutes

Lesson

- Begin by having students hold up a shape as you call out its name to check for shape recognition.

- Now ask students if they can combine two triangles to form a rectangle.

- Try combining two squares to make a rectangle.

- How about a square and two triangles to make a larger triangle.

- Continue as desired.

Assessment: Correct creation of shapes

K.G.6: Lesson Two

Title: Follow the Pattern

Topic: Combining shapes into new shapes

Objective of lesson: Students will combine shapes to form new shapes

Common Core State Standard used: K.G:6: Compose simple shapes to form larger shapes

Materials Needed

Pattern blocks

Shape designs (Sample included)

Time for Lesson: 5 minutes

Lesson

- Explain to students that blocks can be used to create bigger pictures
- Share pattern block cards with students.
- Allow students to create the picture from pattern blocks

Assessment: Correct completion of pattern pictures.